Underground and Independent Rap

(an appreciation for insiders and a glimpse for outsiders)

Zachary Scribe

Underground and Independent Rap

©2007 by Zachary Scribe. All rights reserved.

Published by the author/Maelstrom Media. All pieces composed between 2003 and 2007.

First edition.

ISBN 978-0-6151-5349-0

The Table of Contents for Scribe's Book

Preamble 5

Introduction 6

Chapter Ace: The Origins of the Underground Rap Movement 9

Chapter Deuce: I Don't Fuck Around, Therefore You Shouldn't 14

Chapter Trey: Quills and Quanta 27

Chapter Four: On the Trail of the Elusive Hiphop Backpacker 34

Chapter Five: The Fellowship of the Mic 45

Chapter 6: The Annotated Indie-Rap Record Guide 62

Chapter Seven: Pious in the House of the Lord 71

Chapter Octagon: The Praxis of Indie Rap in Online Postmodernist Relativity 76

Chapter 9: What's Wrong (and Right) with Hiphop Shows? 82

Chapter Ten: A Brief Story of Little Consequence 90

Chapter 11: Scribe and Sole Exchange E-Mails Across the Atlantic Ocean 91

Chapter 12: How I Learned to Stop Worrying and Listen to Cage 96

Chapter Thirteen: The Obligatory Collection of Lists 109

Chapter Fourteen: Insert Clever Chapter Title Here 115

Chapter 15: Ten ?s for the Offwhyte MC 120

Chapter Sickteen: Styling 124

Chapter 17: Mandrake and Me   131

Chapter Eighteen: But Seriously, Folks   136

Chapter 19: The Aryan Hiphop Movement   147

Chapter 20: A New Yorker Packs the House in Maine   152

Chapter 21: Sado-Rap   155

Chapter 22: The Bus Ride   160

Chapter 23: Coda   172

Postscript   193

Appendix: An Underground Insider's Glossary for Outsiders   195

Preamble: The Introduction to the Introduction

I guess I shouldn't have written the intro track before the rest of my book; in retrospect it seems rather backwards and would have been a foolish move if it had been undertaken by anyone other than myself. But the burden of genius is heavy, and so I'm going to write a supplemental prologue instead of scrapping the brilliant, original "intro." The book I had intended to assemble was the definitive guide to indie rap, a serious book with bits of humor added for entertainment value. The humor took over, of course, and, besides that, it became more of an opinionated and selective guide for those who don't know about underground rap and an in-joke for those who already know the score. It also became a much more research-heavy, somewhat more complex (by which I mean "meandering"), and longer work than intended. At some point I wondered whether I would ever finish writing and revising this fucking garbage, but (cue Captain Obvious) here it is. Readers must beware that several chapters are pieces of satirical fiction, although these ruses will be revealed at the end of the book for the sake of anyone who suffers from gullibility.

Introduction

I've read a few books since obtaining literacy at the age of six. Some of these tomes have concerned hiphop music, though most have not, which has proved beneficial. While some of these hiphop-related books are certainly good—Ronin Ro's expose of Death Row Records (*Have Gun, Will Travel*), the David Foster Wallace and Marc Costello project *Signifying Rappers*, and a few others come to mind—only three—those written by Jeff Chang (*Can't Stop Won't Stop*), Brian Cross (*It's Not About A Salary*) and Upski Wimsatt (*Bomb the Suburbs*, definitely not its inferior sequel)—qualify as *great* in my estimation, with Chang's the most impressive work I've taken in yet. Still, none that I've read has approached the potential held by hiphop as a topic; after all, hiphop is widely considered the most influential and possibly the most important cultural movement in the United States since rock and roll's heyday, and thus one might reasonably assume that there's a great book to be written, just waiting in there somewhere. Meanwhile Dave Tompkins, Boots Riley, the pedestrian, or anyone else who might possess the talent to compose the Great Hiphop Manifesto is in no hurry to do so.

Therefore I, "the messiah of hiphop" (in the words of the hiphop/electroclash producer Bomarr Monk), have taken it upon myself to do what no other writer has ever done. I am going to present to the Hiphop Nation the definitive book on rap, the magnum opus that will transcend hiphop, earn me vast acclaim and remain in print for centuries after my death. Actually, I have *no* such intention. Rap has become much too broad for anyone to really write a "definitive" treatise on the entire phenomenon without sacrificing the depth of insight that makes books worthwhile. Furthermore, I have little interest in covering

Run-DMC and other Old School acts (the rap records released prior to 1987 have hardly aged well), the many sucky-but-successful mainstream hacks, the talented-but-overexposed mainstream artists, or anyone other than the rappers and producers who have dragged hiphop music along the path to musical credibility. What I really want to channel is *the* book on underground rap. The one that talks about all of the indie/DIY types who have languished in obscurity for n years and have continued to advance the form of self-expression designated as hiphop music. Aside from Cross's *It's Not About A Salary*, there is no tome a reader can find at a library or a book store or a record store and learn of the Los Angeles underground scene that spawned such luminaries as Freestyle Fellowship and Volume 10. And there is no book to be found on more recent developments like Cincinnati's Scribble Jam, the eclectic record label and artist collective Anticon, or the rise of many small scenes in such boondocks towns as Portland, ME, and Lawrence, KS. Other than a few mediocre magazines, Tower Records or Waldenbooks can't offer anything about the likes of Pharoahe Monch and Busdriver, which is rather unfortunate because, I believe, the work of some of the finest writers in the US and Canada today is to be found on rap recordings, not necessarily in a paperback from HarperCollins or in a literary periodical. And some of the most innovative musicianship and music production are coming from guys who are unlikely ever to get the fame and respect of the Neptunez or Phil Spector.

Though I'm only 26 years old as I type this, I've been a writer for as long as I can remember and a hiphop fan almost as long. Rap is one of the few obsessions in my life. Hence, while my ability to write the Great Hiphop Book has yet to be determined, I qualify for, at least, an attempt at it. And, yes, I am a friend, acquaintance, or former friend or acquaintance of some of the human subjects treated herein; but I have no plans to fall victim to Nelson George Syndrome. And, yes, I rap and produce; but hype about my own work will not be found anywhere in this publication. I am a genius—of this I am certain—and so if you (the reader) cannot understand some sections or fail to recognize when I'm being satirical and when I'm being sincere, then perhaps you'd be better served by a less challenging publication, such as the latest hack work by Dan Brown or *The Source* or the memoirs of a professional wrestler or even a children's book. Just don't expect me to sacrifice humor for the sake of simplicity or literal truth. And I will never fall the fuck off, I promise.

Chapter Ace: The Origins of the Underground Rap Movement

"During these last decades the interest in professional fasting has markedly diminished." (Franz Kafka, "A Hunger Artist")

By the late 1980s hiphop music had ascended from the depths of commercial obscurity and critical indifference to claim some measure of respect. Several New York and Los Angeles groups (such as Public Enemy and N.W.A.) had gold or platinum plaques, MTV had *Yo! MTV Raps*, a show devoted to hiphop videos, and some non-idiots had taken notice of the vocal and lyrical talent and innovative production of such artists as Rakim, De La Soul, and the Ultramagnetic MCs. Unfortunately, the burgeoning commercial success, with its now-obvious potential for massive growth, would soon conflict with the maturation of the music itself. There is greater profit potential in entertainment than in art, and the decision by the major labels to aggressively market hacks like Warren G and to ignore virtuosos like Pharoahe Monch should surprise no one familiar with the history of the rock 'n' roll business. (Of course, this decision was undoubtedly influenced by something beyond the accessibility of their respective musical outputs; of these two, the one who briefly achieved household-name status was considerably more photogenic than his obscure contemporary.) But the discerning hiphoppers' appetite for progression was not whetted by those corporate releases wherein good quality was an unexpected bonus. Hence the establishment in the '90s of DIY scenes and independent labels, which, in the absence of genuine concern for quality at the major labels[1], would foster the continued growth of rap as an auditory art form.

The present author is hardly qualified to cover the entire history of every local

---

[1] Rapper and occasional essayist Nate Mezmer contributed an excellent piece ("187 Proof," published on April 14, 2006) to the radical online newsmagazine (and possible greatest Web site ever) *Counterpunch* (www.counterpunch.org) that laments the "lack of lyrical credibility as well as social value" in most rap songs polluting the commercial air waves these days. I think he summarizes the situation as well as I could.

scene, the national movement, and the international implications; in fact, no one, as far as I know, is qualified for such an endeavor. In the absence of such an overview, a few specific examples should provide the unitiated reader with a good idea of what this whole obscure-rap phenomenon is like. So here we go...

Around the time that Tone Loc was riding rock riffs and catchy choruses on the road to mainstream success, some fellow Californians were forming a scene centered at a weekly open mic event in Los Angeles. Project Blowed would be directly or indirectly inspirational for countless innovators on the West Coast (and elsewhere, to a lesser extent), which makes its best-known location noteworthy; the Good Life, apparently a health-food store by day, was transformed on Thursdays into a venue for some of the most advanced vocalism known to humankind. These motherfuckers weren't getting rich from performing at the Blowed—their love for the music and desire to share their contributions to it with others drove them to galvanize the microphone with wig-splitting wordplay and vocal gymnastics.

Back in 1996 or thereabouts Slug and Ant (the rapper and producer who comprise the Twin Cities titan Atmosphere) created a "four-track fiasco" entitled "God's Bathroom Floor," released on Atmosphere's *Overcast!* EP. Recorded on equipment closer to a Fisher Price tape deck than to the modern 48-track studio, it nonetheless stands as a rap classic on the strength of a jazzy loop, Ant's solid beat, Slug's distinct delivery, and an amalgam of emotive lyrics. A work of this quality requires no gleaming studio, no famous engineer, and no marketing strategy. Check the flow, Sean's got nice styles.

The oddball label/collective Anticon, in its early days, recorded on equipment kept first in producer Moodswing's bedroom and then in the pedestrian's bedroom, both of which were in the lower level of a cheap Oakland duplex that at various times also housed Sole, Dose, Alias, DJ Mayonnaise, and Octavious. Some of the tracks laid down there found their way to Sole's *Bottle of Humans*,

Themselves' *Them*, and the Mush Records compilation *Ropeladder 12*; discriminating music fans around the planet would come to memorize lyrics and nod heads to songs recorded next to some guy's bed.

In Portland, Maine, in 2004, while I was working on the present book, the Seattle-based crew Oldominion came to town for a show. I had met Sleep, the foremost member of the group, about four years beforehand and assumed he wouldn't remember my inconsequential ass. Wrong—he recalled, with surprising detail, chatting with me in East Oakland when he and his partners came to the Bay for a show and Sole introduced us. Sleep agreed to answer some questions for my book.[2], and then we smoked ganja in the parking lot next to the venue. That was the kind of Sixties-throwback encounter that wouldn't have occurred if Sleep had been a major-label artist or if I had been a corporate journalist.

A certain rapper and I were in need of marijuana one day in 1998 or '99. For whatever reason, I had no steady merchant at the time, but he had linked with someone who supposedly had some good green; hence we headed over to this dude's pad (in West Oakland, if I remember correctly). At some point before we arrived there my man informed me that the guy we were buying ganja from was a producer of some esteem in the Bay Area's DIY- and indie-rap scene. We

---

[2] In this interview Sleep admitted to sporting Cross Colors gear back in the day (for our age bracket that generally means the early-to-mid-1990s) and added that he rocked polka dots (a fashion decision I had made myself) as well. (If I could attach a sub-footnote with this word-processing software I would mention that Sole has frequently claimed that he and Alias met in the same era at a mall when they admired each other's Cross Colors threads; if I could add a sub-sub-footnote I would note that my good friend Ben and I met at a college class in 1997 when we liked each other's Wu-Tang Clan shirts.)

later procured 'shrooms from this same dude, who apparently supported his musical efforts with such commerce. (Maybe a year later my man and I would go through another Bay Area indie-rap head, this time a rapper who told me he paid for his collegiate textbooks this way.) To paraphrase El-Producto, an indie-rap artist is going to get his record out even if he has to sell a bucket of weed to finance it.

On the other hand, Gift of Gab, one half of Northern Cali's Blackalicious, somehow got one of his songs onto a TV commercial for Volvo or Pepsi or something in 2004, Buck65 signed a deal with Time-Warner's Canadian division a few years ago, you can find Sage Francis CDs in chain stores across the United States, and a couple members of the Def Jux roster had songs featured on a mass-marketed Playstation football game (called *ESPN NFL 2K5*) late in '04. And those are just a few examples of mainstream recognition that happen to come to mind right now.

One should not be fooled, of course. I once heard Boots Riley, in a radio interview, admit that he was so broke during the mid-Nineties that he suffered from malnourishment--and that was while the Coup was signed to Wild Pitch, a label with major distribution. Gift of Gab and Chief Xcel are probably not raking in the dollars just yet. I attended a Buck65 performance in Maine in '04 (in support of his major-label debut) that, despite its relatively small venue, failed to sell out; his fiance worked the merchandise table for him. Sage Francis only recently got health insurance. If one were to ask the average fan of, say, Lil Jon or Eminem if he or she had ever heard of Aesoprock, a blank stare would be the most probable response.

Of course, underground rap acts who achieve some sort of mainstream success (usually in the form of a major-label contract) understand, albeit to differing extents, the nature of the record industry's economic structure and the rigidity of the USA's class system. I doubt that they assume that fortune and fame are in their future, right around the proverbial corner. But the opportunity to become a professional musician is not easy to reject, and I admire those willing to attempt the improbable. And for those who get dropped after failing to move a million units as well as those who know that they will enjoy greater creative control and, usually, more money by either doing it themselves or hooking up with a minor label, we have the vaults of the vaunted underground.

The following visual aid is provided for those who are unfamiliar with rap's heirarchy.

The Six Spheres of Hiphop Authenticity

On the graph below one can see clearly illustrated the six concentric ellipses—slated for an expansion and re-alignment as nine circles in 2010—of hiphop fame and its inverse relation to perceived authenticity. The innermost circle (1) is DIY obscurity. (2) represents underground respect; (3) stands for indie-label credentials. (4) intersects with (3) and (5) and signifies a combination of indie cred and major-label validity. (5) means minor stardom, whereas (6) means major stardom.

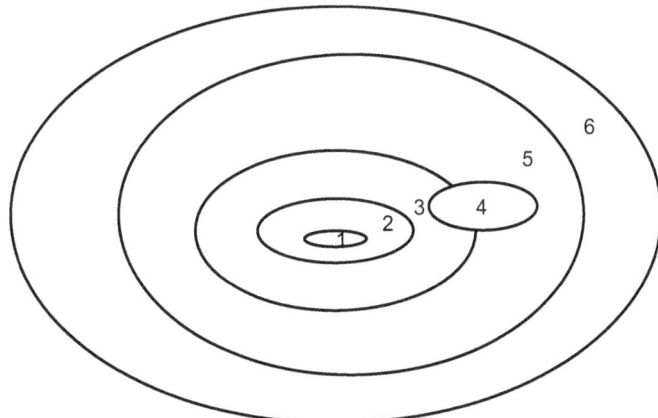

Chapter Deuce: I Don't Fuck Around, Therefore You Shouldn't

Let's get down to business. I don't got time to play around. What is this? A continuation of the gratuitously long and overly explanatory introduction? No. How about accounts of some of my favorite "hiphop moments" since the age of nine? Right on. After all, what could better fit a purportedly nonfiction book purportedly about hiphop than the very hiphop-centric author's own experiences? Furthermore, almost any excuse for an indulgence in autobiography proves irresistible to the egotistical windbags, of whom I am one, who isolate themselves for hours at a time and commit their self-important blather to paper or PC. I'm not going platinum; I'm going double-uranium.[3]

I was born in the year of the snake, when two sevens clashed and rap was forged in the riot fires of the Bronx. At the tender age of eight or nine, while in the early years of what would become a long tenure in the decidedly non-hiphop town of Standish, Maine, a pair of videos on MTV provided my first exposure to rap. Of course, I can't remember much in the way of details, given the time that has passed, but I remember clearly that I was amazed at what I saw. These two songs were probably the first rap tracks I'd ever heard, and the sonic contrast with the popular songs I'd already been exposed to was profound. The Beastie Boys' "Fight For Your Right to Party" and Run-DMC's "It's Tricky," compared to something from Bon Jovi or Michael Jackson, were assaults of raw rhythm and vocal cadence. Then there was the aggressive posturing in the videos. And the no-nonsense b-boy clothing. It was the total package, really, that captivated my senses back in '86 or '87.

My aunt Pia was cool enough to give me a Beastie Boys tape for my tenth

---

[3] My apologies, Mr. Chappelle.

birthday in 1987; I still have it. I played the fuck out of that cassette for a couple years and along the way used my weekly allowance on occasion to save up for a new rap tape instead of baseball cards or comic books. I really liked DJ Jazzy Jeff and the Fresh Prince.

Sure, I can hardly get nostalgic for the likes of Hammer and Young MC, but during the summer between elementary school and junior high school I purchased a recording that would split my wig—Public Enemy's "Welcome to the Terrordome." Wow. That was intense ish for a twelve-year-old kid, even a smart one. Kind of like being smacked upside the head musically. And that, of course, would be my second big hiphop moment.

Anyway, several years passed while my hiphop obsession continued, and in 1994, during my sophomore year in high school[4], I decided I might try to become an emcee. I scribbled crappy lyrics, mostly battle rhymes, during boring classes and practiced them in my bedroom when no one else was home. How much skill did I have back then? "You've been sleeping, and the alarm went off." "You tried to take a shot but you missed/ like Shaquille on the foul line/ you can't take what's mine." Yup, I'm sure Nas would have been quaking in his Timberlands if he had witnessed an onslaught of such lyrical intensity during the *Illmatic* era.

Regardless, during the summer after my high school graduation I felt compelled to get serious about becoming a rapper. I wrote my first songs,

---

[4] I attended Bonny Eagle High School, an odd assemblage of teenaged flotsam and jetsam that also saw Alias, DJ Mayonnaise, and, briefly, JD Walker. In my interview with him Alias offered, "I think Bonny Eagle is the only place where I've ever seen a physical altercation when the two guys got up afterwards, shook hands, and walked away. I've never seen that anywhere else, and I think that's the only place where I ever will see that."

injecting them with the oddball humor and radical politics that my unfortunate high-school classmates had come to know me by. And it was then, in the heat of the '96 electoral campaigns, that I composed my signature piece—"Fuck the G.O.P." At 18 I had written the stupendously bad song that haunts me to this day, and the events surrounding it comprise my next hiphop memory; this was indie rap at its best and worst. (Warning: the following anecdote is one among several which, along with many other passages herein, are intended to add humor to this work, thereby both increasing the entertainment value for the reader and further inflating the author's aggrandized views of his capacity for wit. Like everything else in this book, it can be safely ignored.)

"Fuck the G.O.P.," of course, is a diatribe inspired by NWA's "Fuck the Police" and directed against the arch-conservative wing of the Republican Party. Thus building on such subtle lines as "Bob Dole, another Republican asshole," and armed with my still-developing, awkward, off-beat "flow," I completed a classic of underground godawfulness in the spring of 1997. Assured that heads would appreciate the honesty and integrity of my self-produced jam and overlook its, um, less-polished aspects, I actually undertook the effort and the expense of professionally recording, mixing, and duplicating this song for mass consumption.

I spent untold hours and a few hundred dollars getting my tape (which included a b-side called "Save the Humans") out there. Then my opus was roundly dissed, ignored, and ridiculed (one anonymous poster on an Internet message board described my vocal style as a Saafir-Chuck D hybrid on crack, smack, or glue), and many who heard the song are unlikely to ever appreciate my later-period music because they will always associate me with one of the worst songs they've ever heard. And we're not even going to discuss the self-designed tape cover.⁵ So why did I write just one paragraph previous that "Fuck the GOP" embodies/embodied the *best* as well as the worst aspects of the underground scene? Well, not one fucking businessman controlled any aspect of the product; I used my own money, a result of my personal passion for the whole venture. Also, I wrote, produced (with a little assistance from DJ Mindwrecker and the Grey Hermit in the studio⁶), performed, graphically designed, and promoted the cassette myself, in true DIY fashion. How many major-label releases can boast such a commitment? Furthermore, despite all of my liberal-reformist naiveté, I spoke on socio-economic issues at a time when no well-known MC did. And, finally, I parleyed the entire fiasco into a way to meet other youths involved in the underground rap scene, and, essentially, almost every contact that I've made since recording those two songs has descended from the connections I made in 1997. That's the way the underground tends to work.

Fast-forward one year. I found myself in San Francisco for the summer⁷

---

⁵ OK, if you insist on learning about it, I illustrated the damn thing myself, and I seriously cannot draw any better than that. My development as a visual artist halted in the second grade, and if you were to see the pictures of Godzilla I drew back then you'd see the same infantile style that spawned my G.O.P. elephant. I don't know what the frig I was thinking when I went ahead with that tape cover.

⁶ For the sake of humor, I wish I had a video of these guys and the engineer in the studio as they attempted to coach me into staying on beat; it would have preserved for posterity statements like "Scribe, the end of the Phil Gramm line is hitting after the beat" and "you really need to keep the same cadence for the whole verse".

⁷ See chapter 22 for the prelude to this.

(actually my stay in the Bay Area got extended to 5½ years, but that's irrelevant to this story), working a thankless retail job and hanging out with some cool mutherfuckers. In early July Sole returned from a week or two spent in the Midwest, where he performed at a few places and recorded some project with the recently-renamed Alias (formerly known as Bren the Microphone Wrecker and then Mysterious), Slug of Atmosphere (who was responsible for "Scapegoat," my favorite cut that spring), some MC from Cincinnati named DoseOne, and a few producers. I talked to Sole from the payphone in the hostel I stayed at, and he was very excited about the songs the four of them had done ("dude, this is the best music I've ever made"). Feeling skeptical, I hiked up to the apartment building where he sublet a room and sat politely to listen. He hit the play and record buttons so that I could simultaneously hear and get a copy of the unmixed version of this "supergroup" album, and I was immediately floored by Deep Puddle Dynamics. I had made some mostly awkward attempts at philosophical, poetic, and autobiographical lyricism myself—and these guys weren't the first to explore emotive rap—but this quartet demonstrated just how amazing such an undertaking could be when carried out by emcees with actual skills. Alias had become great, practically overnight, and the other three had elevated their respective levels of vocal and lyrical prowess. Don't front on the production, either. Among the original Deep Puddle Dynamics songs was a never-finished track called "Metaphors," in which each MC spit an extended metaphor that made no direct reference to its signifier and Slug and Sole intoned "yo, dun, your similes is killing me" while Alias and Dose, respectively, chanted "are you" and "like" on other vocal tracks for a should-have-been-classic chorus. I played this dub, along with Volume10's album, Freestyle Fellowship's *To Whom It May Concern*, a Ras Kass rarities compilation, and one of Dose's homemade *Hemispheres* tapes (the ones with mysterious radio background noise at the end of each side and a special Why?-illustrated cover) incessantly for the rest of the summer. I bumped nothing but underground rap and Fiona Apple (who, I was sure, I would meet and convince to fall in love with me) in my Walkman in those days. A record label called Anticon began to take shape, but that's a long and separate story that I don't feel qualified to tell.

For now let's revisit the middle of August, 1999, and the city of Cincinnati, home of the three-day, festival-like Scribble Jam. Pumped from a few months of daily freestyle practice, I was intent on entering the MC battle; but regardless of that event's outcome, I knew I would have a good time that weekend. I crashed at the three-bedroom apartment shared by Dose, Why?, and Odd Nosdam, and I wasn't the only one; if I remember right, DJ Signify, Ade Em, Shalem, Sole[8], a friend of Sole's from Maine named Joe, a Dj from Detroit named Rus, Adverse, Scott Matelik, Labtekwon and his two friends whose names I've forgotten and I'm not sure who else also slept there, which was certainly better than a hotel.

Hundreds or maybe a couple of thousand heads who were into this beneath-the-surface rap shit gathered in the muggy (I had never experienced such humidity) city on the river, and things started popping from the first night. Several rappers, too eager or anxious to wait for the next day's battles, had formed a cipher outside the club where several acts were slated to perform, and the circle got heated. When I noticed who was involved, I strutted over and took a spot maybe two heads from the center of the circle. What I witnessed was captured only by a few video cameras and the eyes of those there at that moment. The vaunted P.E.A.C.E. of Freestyle Fellowship battled Prime of Chicago's Molemen crew, Ade Em of the 1200 Hobos (and New Hampshire, of

---

[8] Sole's uncanny manipulation of a car-rental agent who let him rent a car despite the well-established company policy of never renting a car to anyone under the age of twenty-five (Sole was then only twenty-one) astounds me in retrospect.

all places), and DoseOne. Dose, if I remember correctly, used a vocal style that incorporated a rising scale of notes, which impressed P.E.A.C.E. (fuck it, I don't know if his name is really an acronym and definitely don't feel like typing all that shit anymore; from now on it's Peace). Again I'm not sure if I recall correctly, but I think Prime held his own but kinda lost to Peace. Then came the most entertaining part: Ade Em ripped Peace, who probably had never heard of the dude before. The New Englander teased the Los Angeleno about his need for braces and his crappy lyrical contribution to the otherwise-brilliant and then-unreleased Fellowship reunion mini-album (now known as *Shockadoom* but then untitled), and the cipher ended soon thereafter with all witnesses agreeing that the defending Scribble Jam champion had served yet another victim.

Saturday was the much-anticipated day of official competition. I don't remember the DJ battle and paid no attention to the b-boy contest, so we can proceed without delay to the emcee tournament. Hmm, let's see...oh yeah, I sucked and failed to advance beyond the qualifying round. Illogic didn't go far, Slug, Labtek, and Prime chose not to compete, Deuce Leader was as wack as ever, the '97 champ Juice's rumored appearance never materialized, and Keith Murray's younger brother showed up with some written rhymes that were still pretty weak. Peace had come to the Queen City with fellow products of the L.A. scene Otherwise (who apparently was dressed like a Crip) and Abstract Rude, and the three of them did fairly well. Sole dispatched New Yorker Poison Pen by pulling the "you use too many similes" card but got ripped by Otherwise in the next round. Dose hilariously embarrassed a local rapper who lamely reused a couplet from their previous battle on the radio. For all the anticipation of a Dose-Ade Em or Peace-Ade Em match-up, Ade Em got upset early on by somebody named Crescent Moon—I heard someone in the crowd holler "the champ's on the ropes!" while Adam struggled to produce some disses and instead came up with a bizarre little story about how his opponent reminded him of himself. Dose clearly ripped Ab Rude, who was hardly a renowned battler but still decided to complain about the judges' decision. When the smoke cleared we had a final four before us of Dose, Peace, Otherwise, and Minnesota's Eyedea. The Dose-Peace battle was one of the most amazing performances I've ever seen, with the two gifted vocalists using everything they had, but in the end Peace's theatrical stuff, including a few lines that he spit after intentionally dropping the microphone on the floor, gave him a slight edge. Meanwhile the teenaged Eyedea served Otherwise to set up a title bout with a certain buck-toothed Californian. Now came the confusion and conjecture and whatnot. Eyedea and Peace battled intensely, and no one in the audience seemed clear on who was the victor; as it turned out, the judges weren't so sure, either, and the pair of MCs had to go at it again to determine the winner. Eyedea punched below the belt with a reference to Freestyle Fellowship's getting dropped by Island Records after their 1993 album failed to scorch the charts, but aside from that insult and a mention of the crappiness of Peace's best-known song ("Six-Tray," a joint about drive-by shootings) he had nothing to counter Peace's onslaught. As far as this audience member was concerned, Peace was the winner in a close call; he had pulled out several impressive vocal styles, whereas Mikey had stuck to the same flow he had used all night. The judges failed to see things my way, and Eyedea was declared the new Scribble Jam champion.

 The only memory I have from the next day is of Sluggo doing a free solo set in a local park, even operating the Minidisc or DAT player himself to provide the beats. It was the first time I saw Sean Daly perform, and the man exuded charisma and showed an obvious mastery of his lyrics. But my recollection of the next year's Jam isn't nearly as fond, as I again sucked in the preliminary round of the MC battle, was disappointed with the battles (which a partially-disguised Sage Francis won against Ohio native Blueprint), and remember enjoying my only moment in the spotlight (when I gave a half-serious speech for my "campaign for President") and the Sebutones show on Monday night (there was a sort of Anticon showcase the night after Scribble Jam's official conclusion). But I guess nothing is as fun the second time around.

With the nation in the grip of premillennial tension and Y2K-glitch fear, in late 1999 I somehow managed to convince a show promoter from Pittsburg (not to be confused with Pittsburgh), a small city maybe forty-five minutes from Oaktown, to include me in a show that featured some of the Anticonians and assorted Bay Area talent. Some kind of confusion ensued in the time between when the promoter said he'd put me on and the actual night of the show; in short, one of the two dudes who was putting on the show didn't inform the other that I was part of the roster, and I ended up squeezed in for a five-minute set. Feeling, um, "perturbed" at this development, I scrapped my plans to perform any of the "real" songs I had practiced for the show and opted to do "Fuck the GOP" instead. However, I did not change my mind about giving the audience the full Scribe experience and thus took the stage with my recently-purchased U.S.A. flag. I kicked about half of the lyrics from my trademark track, pulled the flag out, and (more or less) desecrated it. I had intended to save this routine for my performance of my brand-new song "Fuck Government" (itself a product of my burgeoning anarchist philosophy) but, given my time constraints, felt compelled to simulate pissing on the Stars and Stripes. At least one dude in the audience was offended, claiming his father was a war veteran, and when I tossed the symbolically soiled fabric into the crowd he took it. We had an argument when I got off the stage, and he walked off into the suburban night with the flag draped on his shoulders (feeling vindicated, I suppose).

That incident barely deviated from the usual somewhat impulsive, slightly reckless, aggressive behavior of my early twenties—I am a calmer 28 as I type this— a period which included an argument with an MC duo at a large indie-rap show in San Fran that nearly escalated to violence, disagreements with neighbors that nearly escalated to violence, spats with housemates that escalated to yelling and minor violence, obsessive solitary freestyling sessions, frequent reading of Chomsky, prolific lyricizing, three resignations from the same job (all of them retracted soon after), a few mushroom trips and other substance experiences, Napster-enabled file-trading madness, some rhyme battles, some wack performances I gave the public, a freelance article on the Stuffed Animals project that was shot down by the *SF Weekly* music editor, a jaw broken because I stood my ground instead of fleeing when faced with an armed, angry, irrational man, a brief foray into graffiti, umpteen housing changes (my four-track recorder, Yamaha sampler, and rhyme book in tow every time), an abortive attempt to write for *The Source Online*, and numerous similar bits of personal historical context, some of which I'd prefer my parents not to read about.

Thus seen through a wide-angle lens, encompassing the total panorama of my life at the time, my personal Internet flame war fit in nicely. Though my full-length DIY tape *Marxist Catharsis* failed to set the world ablaze in 1999, I held out hope in the year 2G that the Hiphop Nation would appreciate my compositions and in 2000 came, along with the vindication of my year-old predictions that the stock market would crash and Bush and Gore would face each other in November, *Purgatory,* my first CD, another DIY product available only at two Bay Area record stores. By the spring of 2001 I had long since begun work on a sequel but still wanted an online retailer to carry *Purgatory*. Almost no one would sell it because it lacked shrink wrap (a decision I had made to save waste, not money), but one webmaster decided to give a staffer my disc for review. The one-star rating this critic offered was harsh but forgivable; the absurd and personally insulting review that accompanied it was not. I posted an angry response on one of the site's message boards, prompting a nasty war of words, which included some friends who took my side and some boneheads from cyberspace and which must have lasted a week. Two years later the webmaster, despite apparently brisk sales of merchandise, opted to shut down the entire site and run for a seat in Congress. Seriously. A number of furious customers accused that business of stiffing them after taking payment on their last orders. Seriously. So the site, which I'll call "hiphopeternity.com" to avoid any potential accusations of libel, waved its middlefinger at us on its way into oblivion.

January of 2002 brought both a new calendar and a fresh slate of opportunities for me to make a spectacle of myself. The potential dangers of alcohol abuse are well known, and sports spectatorship compounds the risks, which can ramp up when chased with a cocktail of indie-rap acts. So on a Saturday that promised beer, football, and rap for young Scribe, I sat at home and watched my Raiders get robbed of victory by some officials (tuck rule? that was a fucking fumble, and you can put that on my tombstone) in the so-called Snow Bowl; I poured micro-brew beers down my throat for over three hours, becoming drunk and belligerent by the time the Patriots were handed a fraudulent playoff win. Not too bent to go out, I stuck to the script and caught the train from Berkeley to San Francisco for a promising show.

When I arrived at the club the two friends I was supposed to meet inside were stuck outside, as one of them lacked a ticket to the newly sold-out show. I had no ticket myself, yet the three of us, in a manner lost amid the fog of old memories, somehow finagled our way in. I immediately stepped to the bar and ordered a drink to sip while the opening act, which I think was Of Mexican Descent, took the stage and I conversed with some friendly audience members. Busdriver made an unbilled cameo, and I decided I should try to find him after the show for a little repartee. Or maybe some chit-chat. Definitely not jibber-jabber, though. I had another drink and sat on a bar stool while Sole performed, followed by Sage Francis[9], unless it was the other way around. At some point I stumbled to the club's perch-like upper level, which offered tables and a clear view of the stage, and quickly passed out. After an unknown interval I awoke with an obvious need to vomit, hurried downstairs to the bathroom, found the only toilet occupied, and purged into the sink. I returned to the upstairs spot and passed out at another table. (Why my drunken ass was not tossed out of the place remains a mystery.) Eventually an employee shook me awake to inform me that the show was over and the venue was closing. I dragged myself outside to hook up with my boys, noticed Busdriver nearby, and decided I—drunkenness be damned— should meet the man. I can hardly speculate on how inebriated I must have appeared to him, but Bus' treated me with undue respect and even accepted a copy of my then-new CD (*Extended Play*). I never was able to speak with Busdriver again, but I hope that: a) the CD-R I gave him was not among those that I later learned had skips; b) I didn't leave a ridiculous, asinine impression. I, of course, failed to learn anything important in the aftermath of my public display of insobriety, continuing to drink frequently, occasionally to the extent of a binge, which sometimes involved puking or passing out in public, until I induced a couple of minor blackouts and finally decided in 2006 I'd had my fill of alcohol. I usually drink in moderation and mostly on very special occasions now, and if I ever need a reminder of how badly booze can fuck up your life I can simply call my sister, the recovering alcoholic; the reader may have to settle for a good cautionary tale like mine or Gift of Gab's ("40 oz for Breakfast,"on Blackalicous's *Melodica*) or Slug's ("Pour Me Another," from Atmosphere's *You Can't Believe How Much Fun We're Having*). Regardless of its presence at most of the venues where indie

---

[9] Hey, Paul, the Masters aren't back. They never left.

rappers and DJs ply their trade, alcohol is not something to be consumed in a cavalier fashion and is certainly not an inevitable part of the culture.

Therefore, I declare, live it up. But, when seizing the day and fighting the power to a hiphop soundtrack, use some sense because there is almost definitely no afterlife; or, alternately, if space-time is curved sufficiently or if Nietzsche was correct in positing an Eternal Return then we all have to not only live with our actions but live with them infinitely.

Chapter Trey: Quills and Quanta

At this point few hiphop musicians or fans would suggest any sort of grand unified definition of the musical form is necessary—and it may prove impossible if attempted. How can anyone define a genre that includes Too $hort, Rob Swift, Dalek, and Lauryn Hill? Where are the boundaries? Nobody has bothered to establish any, yet we somehow know how to separate hiphop, even the envelope-pushing stuff, from everything else. As with other less-than-concrete concepts like poetry and comedy, we have a general idea of the thing and tend to recognize it when we encounter it. Certainly, some artists test the limits, but we can usually pin them down at some point.

More difficult than the designation of "hiphop" or "rap" is that dodgy description, "underground" or "indie." Usually it's easy to separate obscure (Kabir) from popular (The Game), but when the line is blurred (O.C.) I have to decide, in what may seem like an arbitrary manner, how much financial success and mainstream publicity a given soloist or group has enjoyed. For example, how much attention did the Digable Planets get when they were releasing records through a division of Elektra? Did they frequent the Lyricist Lounge, affiliate themselves with college radio, or book their own tours? Rather than tying myself in obsessive knots over categorization, I decided long ago to simply go with my gut feeling on who to include in this book.

Further, taking any approach to a discussion of hiphop music that ignores its connections to other types of music would be foolish. After all, rap has utilized samples so often and so brilliantly for so long that the progress of its instrumental production has intertwined with (though not depended on) the advancement of sampling technology. Hiphop producers have borrowed bits from every available genre, except perhaps polka and bluegrass, and they have used a variety of hardware whose circuitry was made possible by the field of physics called quantum mechanics.

Quantum mechanics, of course, deals in atoms, subatomic particles and waves, and it has, among many other things, helped to give us such tools as lasers. Laser equipment reads the music encoded on compact discs at something like the speed of light—the speed of lasers varies—and no rapper, no matter how nimble of tongue, can ever rap more rapidly than the velocity of a laser beam. Yes, South Bronx legend Percee P[10] spits most of his rhymes at a clip that must overwhelm the auditory processors of all but the best-trained rap listeners, but even the sound waves he emits cannot, even given some superhuman vocal ability, move faster than light. In fact, even if he or someone else, such as fellow fast-rap pioneer Spoon Iodine, were to attempt to move their mouths at a superhuman speed, they would presumably cause a sonic boom when their lips exceeded the speed of sound and thus thunderously drown out the beat while still at a small fraction of the speed of light.

Still, some may object that ways to cheat the light-speed barrier have been theorized by physicists for many years, and indeed the famous "wormholes" popularized by science fiction authors and actual scientists alike offer a hypothetical means of time travel or incredibly fast space travel, skeptics continue to hold sway, perhaps typified by physicist Jim Al-Khalili's statement, among descriptions of possible ways to travel through time, that he believes the most likely reality is that "[t]ime travel

---

[10] For example, on his 1989 collaboration with Ekim "Lung Collapsing Lyrics" or on "A Day at the Races," his cameo on the Jurassic 5 LP *Power in Numbers* or even on his EP *Put It On the Line*.

to the past is forbidden by some as yet undiscovered law of physics."[11] L.A. underground denizen Circus postulates, "maybe aliens are just time travellers from the future"[12]; however, both Al-Khalili[13] and Stephen Hawking[14] cast serious doubt on this idea, one with "the something-from-nothing paradox" and the other with "the chronology protection conjecture." Also, the 3 Melancholy Gypsies (Scarub, Eligh, and Murs) might be disappointed, if they earnestly believe in the extraterrestrial visitors they discuss in "Landing," from *Grand Caravan to the Rim of the World*, for these physicists reveal that the massive distance between Earth and the nearest neighboring solar system makes alien visitation implausible.

But back to the lecture at hand. Percee P has been recording sporadically for nearly two decades, yet this output has not culminated in an actual album. Clearly, his perception of time must be less linear than the average person's, or, at least, he takes a long view of history and understands that two decades of our time will seem little different from two weeks to our descendants. After all, who among us cares how long Cicero or Sun Tzu needed to complete their respective magnum opuses? The Rhyme Inspector entitles one EP *Throwback Rap Attack*, most likely because he is taking his audience on a brief reminiscence (hence "throwback"), and he certainly attacks the molecules of oxygen and carbon in his immediate surroundings, a bit like a particle accelerator smashing atoms together at high speeds. Though he rarely

---

[11] *Black Holes, Wormholes & Time Machines* (1999), p. 192.

[12] "We Are Not Alone," from *Gawd Bless the Faceless Cowards*.

[13] Ibid., p. 183.

[14] In the tenth anniversary edition of *A Brief History of Time*, p. 169.

reaches the ridiculous velocities achieved by his counterparts out West, he does batter beats at a tempo much higher than anything attempted by most of his contemporaries. This three-song set almost suggests a man who is trying symbolically to move backward in time ("throwback") through some means involving sound waves ("rap") and smashed atoms ("attack").

If by no other means, Percee does help establish a direct link with a previous time and place, namely the 1960s-70s progressive-psychedelic rock scene through his collaboration with Edan on the latter's *Beauty and the Beat*. Their song interpolates a sample from *The Dark Side of the Moon*, adding them to the short list of known Floyd loop-rockers, alongside Cage and Tame1—the Leak Brothers' album flips samples from the same album—as well as Buck65, who uses "Careful with that Axe, Eugene" on *Vertex*.

Heavy rock band Clutch titled a song on *Pure Rock Fury* "Careful with that Mic," presumably in homage to Floyd, and twenty or thirty years hence Clutch may find its riffage or percussion sampled by avant-garde rappers who are only babies as I write this. Those future musicians also may perform in the ruins of some ancient empire, much as the members of that post-empire British band Floyd played among decaying Roman antiques for the film *Live at Pompeii*. Persian ruins might make a fitting location for this future concert movie, especially if this hypothetical group hails from a U.S. empire in decline.

If wormholes are not real, then those hiphop musicians who seem to traverse the massive gap between underground and mainstream must have encountered some kind of warped space-time. That would explain how Pharoahe Monch enjoyed one hit ("Simon Says," from his only solo album) before returning to obscurity, as his life's geodesic (the curved-by-gravity path in space-time described by Stephen Hawking[15]) briefly exposed him to those who perceive in three dimensions as well as those of us who could see him all along in four dimensions. Such warping might also help us understand how samples from Sun Ra's bizarre cinematic allegory *Space Is the Place* appeared on two indie-label releases during the limbo years between Ra's death and the film's DVD release. Radioinactive centers "Launch Padlock Smithereen" (from *Pyramidi*) on a ditty from the film, and Nobody interpolates synth notes from the score into "Sixth Sense" (off his mostly-instrumental *Soulmates*). Madlib, after the re-release, also sampled the film for the Madvillainy project with MF Doom, an odd figure who enjoys the same sort of devoted, outside-the-radar fanbase as Sun Ra.

The similarities between Ra and "Kool" Keith Thornton, another dude with what some call a "cult following," have, I assume, been noted before, with the most prominent being their claims of extraterrestrial connections; Ra, as described in John Szwed's book *Space Is the Place*, earnestly claimed he had been brought by aliens to Saturn, whereas Kool Keith's discography is replete with cosmic themes, often tongue-in-cheek. His raunchy Dr. Octagon persona proclaims, "I was born on Jupiter," ("Earth People," *Dr. Octagon*) and declares he is "armed with space doodoo pistols." He appears with a phony pompadour for the cover of an album titled *Black Elvis/Lost In Space*, he and his Ultramagnetic brethren are asked to "Bring It Down to Earth" for those who "don't understand" (*The Four Horsemen*), Keith/Octagon and journalist Dave Tompkins present the rapper as a time traveler from a millennium hence for a 1996 interview in *Rap Pages*, and so on. Mr.

---

[15] Ibid., pp. 30-31.

Thornton also must travel along the same space-time warp that connects the mainstream and the underground, considering he has appeared on a platinum album by the electro band The Prodigy and enjoyed the high profile and distribution afforded a release on Dreamworks (the second version of *Dr. Octagon*) but has also released a grip of records on various independent labels.

Quantum mechanics and relativity, which is the field of physics that deals with large-scale phenomena, may also enhance our understanding of other underground/indie hiphop musicians. For example, West Coast heads haven't heard from San Francisco producer Molasses since his excellent five-song EP *Madness* dropped in 1997; he possibly stumbled upon a black hole that sucked him in and inevitably crushed him.[16] The same fate may have befallen old Indelible MC J-Treds shortly after the release of his solo single in the late Nineties.

Also, it has been demonstrated by quantum theory that the act of observation changes the object under observation, even in situations where the observer would not appear to interact with the event under observation; by a similar principle, the published or broadcast commentary on a specific musician or musical scene, even absent any direct interaction with the subject, tends to change that person's or group's self-perception. Further, the publication of the present book can be reasonably expected to affect, through direct and indirect routes, the artists described within, possibly including those who remain unaware of the book's existence.

---

[16] In Errol Morris's documentary *A Brief History of Time* Hawking and other scientists describe a hypothetical astronaut's ordeal inside a black hole: such a person would supposedly undergo a massive slowing in his perception of time and then get obliviated.

Finally, the Uncertainty Principle, which holds that we can get a precisely accurate measurement of either an object's velocity or its position but not both, potentially reveals the reason that we cannot know the future development of an avant-garde MC, beatsmith, or DJ: once we have pinpointed the given artist's place along his or her progression, the speed and direction of change become unknown.

In conclusion, after many calculations, I believe I have discovered the formula for that rare hiphop record that pleases both the diehard hiphop fanbase and the fickler public at large, e.g. *Illmatic* or *It Takes a Nation of Millions to Hold Us Back*. It is as follows.

$$\Delta = (\Pi \times \Sigma) + \Omega$$

Where Δ is success, Π is talent, Σ is the cosine of perceived authenticity, and Ω is labor.

Chapter Four: On the Trail of the Elusive Hiphop Backpacker

The tale of my search for the legendary (and possibly mythical) creature known as the hiphop backpacker or—as the Native Americans called him—the hootiewah begins as most of my expeditions have begun: with a wager. My fruitless search for a specimen of that much-rumored species known as the abstract rapper had cost me both £50 and the priceless opportunity to wipe the smug look from that bastard Robin Surrey's pock-marked face, although I had privately entertained doubts that I could find the creature in question. However, I later won £100 by locating, in the vast Los Angeles desert, the last surviving member of the Blood and Crip sub-tribes who had collaborated on the epic oral poem Bangin' On Wax. On a similar note, Professor Coopersmith's inability to produce a field recording of the mating call of the spoken-word artist had meant that he had to allow me to ask his wife out for what the Americans call a "fuck date," which she agreed to, which prompted much ribbing of Coopersmith at the Club.

This time around a pittance of £20 was on the line, as well as a shoe polish, a back rub, and a car wash, all personally performed by the loser, not a paid replacement, and I announced at the Club that Lucifer and Beelzebub would be ice skating in their back yards before I'd polish that bastard Robin Surrey's shoes. Before setting out on my trek I placed a call, for morale support, to Professor Best, who, after all, had once proven so many skeptics wrong when he discovered an actual superscientifical rapper in the wild. Best assured me that if anyone were going to find the elusive hiphop backer, then I was the man to do it; he also said—and I haven't known him to be a liar—that, in his professional opinion, there was reason to believe the hootiewah was more than a simple urban legend.

While I had fairly extensive knowledge of the hootiewah already stored in my "dome piece," I knew that I could always use more data on the subject and to that end attempted a bit more research before embarking on my journey. I read reviews of hiphop recordings dating from 1998 to 2002, when interest in the hiphop backpacker peaked, and found a surprising level of hostitility toward the creature, who might not even exist. Had these record reviewers some first-hand experiences with my holy grail? Yes, they must have, because none of these esteemed pundits would ever waste good magazine and newsweekly ink on anything so inconsequential as an urban legend with no basis in fact.

My first act of pre-journey research would be to contact the scribes who had mentioned hootiewahs in their work. No one responded to my e-mails, however, and I turned to my second act of preparatory research, which was contacting a few rappers who had mentioned hiphop backpackers in their lyrics. Slug—he of the Minneapolis, United States, group Atmosphere—had said something on his long-player God Loves Ugly about indie-rap backpackers and presumably had some intimate knowledge of them, perhaps even a personal encounter. I placed a few telly calls and eventually located the man at a recording studio in the so-called Twin Cities.

Thinking I might break the ice with a little levity, I began our conversation by introducing myself and quoting doggerel from one of Slug's better-known songs.

"It ain't me, mutherfucker, it ain't me," I said in the spirit of gentelemanly raillery.

Slug repeated the name of your humble narrator in a querying tone of voice and then stated that he had never heard of me. Then he added that I should never "address [him] in that manner." Our dialogue ended in a rather brusque and unsatisfactory fashion.

Next I would try Eminem, also known as Slim Shady or Marshall Mathers, for he had once "dissed" rivals from a group known as Dilated Peoples by identifying them as a "backpacking, ciphering crew," apparently a high insult in his home town of Detroit, United States. My search never advanced beyond Mr. Mathers's publicist, which was understandable because someone had to prevent strangers like myself from wasting Mathers's valuable time when he could be getting a tattoo while under the influence of one or more of the many narcotics he professes to enjoy.

I, of course, then turned to that duo called Dilated Peoples, only to be informed by their manager that they were too busy recording their "concept" album, the one with the rumored title of Generica, to answer my questions. This was the greatest disappointment yet, as I had expected great insights from Iriscience, the brilliant thinker who had been bold enough to expose the Pope as a Jew in 1998 and also, during an a cappella piece in the D.P. show circa 2000, had taken the controversial stance that war was actually bad, along with something semi-coherent from the other bloke.

Feeling slightly despondent, I pulled an old CD from my collection for my daily drive to the corner store to get a pint of Miller Genuine Draft. Before I started the engine in my auto I skipped to track three of this disc, the debut from an obscure group who called themselves Black Moon, and was astounded to hear the lead vocalist describe his "baggy black jeans, napsack, and beeper." This was amazing! Napsack was a North American term for backpack, and here was one Buckshot Shorty professing to possess one! He must have been a hiphop backpacker, I inferred.

One can easily imagine my renewed disappointment when I finally reached Buckshot himself only to hear him deny any such identity. In fact, he had changed his moniker to Buckshot da B.D. Eye MC, he disavowed records released by his old employer, and he emphatically denied that ownership of a backpack made him a backpacker. Clearly, the time had come for the concrete phase of this search for my quarry.

I purchased a first-class ticket on the next flight from London to New York, booked a room at a four-star hotel in midtown Manhattan (a five-star hotel would have been too upscale for an authentic hiphop adventure), and arranged for a rental town car with a chaffeur. Unfortunately, there were no rap shows in New York City that night, hence I flew out as soon as possible to "scandalous" Los Angeles. By the time of my arrival there it was six in the morning, with no shows to attend there, either. My Negro chaffeur asked around, however, and learned of a show that evening that would feature some local talent.

That night my chaffeur and I made the sojourn to the show, which was somewhere in the vastness of Los Angeles County, and I was entertained by some chubby guys named Awol, 2Mex, and Circus as well as some thinner chaps who called themselves Radio Inactive, Scarub, and Busdriver. A good time was had by all, although I spotted no fans in the audience wearing backpacks. I accosted some of the performers to inquire about the purported phenomenon of the hiphop backpacker, but my slight inebriation must have been noticable because

Awol and Busdriver seemed more interested in being rid of me than in answering my questions. (I think I disguised my British accent quite well, however.) Another dead end on my journey? Perhaps so, but my determination had not wavered.

I caught a flight up to the grand city of San Francisco, where another rap show was slated for a club in the so-called South of Market district. I hadn't been to Baghdad by the Bay since the 1950s and was surprised by the proximity of the drug-addicted hoi polloi to its finer hotels, including the one at which I stayed. This certainly wasn't like London, New York, L.A., or even Chicago, each of which had a larger buffer zone between the rabble and those of us simply trying to enjoy our reasonably-priced, four- or five-star accommodations without the element of grimy, crack-smoking commoners.

Because the night-club in question refused to pay me for the publicity, I refuse to name this establishment until such time as I can get a reasonable sum in return for the business promotion my mention of it would provide; regardless, my latest chaffeur and I entered the venue around 9:20, knowing full well the lack of punctuality among rappers, whether mainstream or underground. A deejay on stage was spinning some recent releases, as the performers hadn't started yet. I glanced around the club, and that's when I spotted my quarry as he came through the door. A hiphop backpacker was here, I was certain, and I wouldn't leave the place without him.

My chauffeur, whose name I cannot recall—as if it were worthy of noting, anyway—stepped outside and nonchalantly strolled to my rental vehicle to move the tranquilizer and the net I would soon require from the trunk to the front seat. I wanted, however, to be sure I had an authentic hiphop backpacker, not a mimic, and thus strutted toward the young man to engage him in a brief conversation.

"What's up wit' it?" I greeted.

"Nuttin', just chillin'," he responded.

He wore a Cannibal Ox tee-shirt, the one that quotes "I want 108 mics" on the back, and I asked what he thought of recent Definitive Juxtaposition releases.

"Well, I've been disappointed with everything the Jukies have put out since last year, especially that last Aesoprock album."

This was exactly the response I expected from a true backpacker and followed with a few more queries, all under the guise of one European's interest in a foreign culture. That was how I learned he no longer listened to Anticon, that he had tapes of radio freestyles performed by Aceyalone and DoseOne that even I didn't have, and that he occasionally "bombed" San Francisco's Muni tunnels and Oakland's train yards with graffiti. In fact, he had some paint cans and fat markers, alongside his Walkman, Zig Zags, and incense, in his backpack at that very moment for post-show activities. I needed great restraint not to reveal my excitement, for I knew that I would soon bag a genuine hiphop backpacker.

I invited my prey and his girlfriend to join my companion and me for some Humbolt County pot in my town car, wherein I had my equipment cleverly concealed by a record-carrying bag of the sort often used by pseudo-deejays for the purpose of attracting young females. Once in the car, I gave the signal to my chaffeur and swiftly turned around to prick the subject in his neck with a tranquilizer-delivering syringe; my partner in this pursuit immediately threw my net over the backpacker. I (literally) kicked the female out of the vehicle, and my rental car accelerated off into the San Francisco night. We had our catch in hand.

Back in England that "mother-fucker" Surrey conceded defeat, and I bathed in the acclaim bestowed upon me by my colleagues in the sciences. In rather obnoxious (but satisfying) fashion, I counted aloud my £20 winnings several times—especially obnoxious because I was paid in two ten-pound notes—while Surrey polished my shoes. Then, standing tall in my newly-shined footwear, I watched Surrey wash my "whip" with a soapy sponge and a garden hose.

Of course, the hootiewah was displayed at our most esteemed anthropology museum in an addition built especially to house my one-of-a-kind specimen, who became something of a sensation on this side of the pond. I was interviewed on TV shows, to which I sometimes brought my safely-shackled backpacker, and wrote one of the most famous scholarly pieces ever published in Europe—I enjoyed both lowbrow celebrity and highbrow respect. The captured animal at first seemed a little melancholy, possibly because of the restrictions inherent to captivity, but he eventually adjusted to his new habitat and now, eighteen months later, seems perfectly content; he has even "tagged" one of the walls in his home and written in a little notebook I provided for him. He spends an hour or two a day playing with the deejay equipment in his bedroom but seems the most joyful when he sees one of his keepers coming to bring him his morning stimulant and antidepressant or his evening sedative and analgesic. I am certain that he is happier here than he would be in the wild and wish that someone would capture a female member of the species so that they might reproduce and stave off extinction.

Chapter Five: The Fellowship of the Mic[17]

Yeah, mutherfucker. If you don't like Freestyle Fellowship, maybe you should skip this chapter. Actually, on second thought, you need to read this ish more than anyone else, fuckface. Because this whole fucking sector of my book is about the Fellowship. That's right. The whole fucking chapter. And maybe I'll give it an orderly structure. But more likely I won't.

Now, I had intended to just write at length about F.F., rambling in my best imitation of what I imagine to be Lester Bangs's style—I've read a bit about Bangs but nothing by him—but then nothing really insightful came to me; and no way in Hell would I write a satirical chapter this time. Anyway, to skip the segue, Hunter Thompson had died recently, I had five bottles of pale ale in me and I was listening to *Shockadoom*, which I first heard as a third-generation dub four years before its actual release. As anyone who's ever been inebriated can tell you, alcohol slows every human function, including thought. Hence I could hardly process the more rapidly delivered verses, even though I'd listened to

---

[17] Get it? That's a reference to J.R.R. Tolkien's whole Hobbit thing.

these songs dozens of times over the years, and Mikah's contribution to "Can You Find...?" was more baffling than ever. What the fuck is he saying? Something about how difficult it is to help a crack fiend to quit, I think. And then I realized I was listening to the next track; not sure what happened to the other three verses and the chorus of that previous song, but I was kinda drunk and didn't care. "Shockadoom," with its rather insistent drum pattern, had me nodding my head, probably offbeat, and I could not follow 95% of the lyrics because it was 3am and I was wasted. "On the Run" was overwhelming, and I was dumbstruck when I heard Self-Jupiter do that weird vocalese bit at the end of his verse. Do I understand what he's saying there when I'm sober? I couldn't recall. By the first strains of the fourth track I'd started staring blankly into space and paying no attention to the music. Clearly, this is not the best way to appreciate the (arguably) best group in rap's oeuvre. I somehow got it together and was somewhat conscious for "We Will Never," my favorite cut on this record. Peace says "you will not hear that sucker shit here, no matter how many joints or beers"; I definitely was on some sucker shit, or, at least, some simpleton shit, after my intake of booze. I needed to sleep or pass out, and the next thing I knew it was noon.

Now it's the next night, in real time, and I've recorded the best recollection of last night's experiment that I can muster. How about consuming a painkiller and then playing Fellowship's masterpiece *Inner City Griots*? Almost any excuse to pop one of the two dozen Vicodin-type pills I have in the kitchen cabinet works for me, and so I swallow a dose of hydrocodone-acetaminophen. I should mention that this is some good stuff, not as good as morphine but certainly comparable to codeine. I play the non-album classic "Umm" and write about last night while I await the "binding to opioid receptors" that simultaneously produces a pleasant sensation and relieves the nearly-constant pain in my mouth caused by my "impacted third molar." Ooh. There it is. I'm slightly dizzy, feeling good all over, but I'm also weak and mentally sluggish. Being a central nervous-system depressant, this narcotic painkiller will have these effects, which are not all that different from those resultant from alcohol. Once again, on most songs the fantastic four emcees are rapping much faster than my impaired brain can handle. This experiment is threatening to become fruitless. I shuffle among the tracks. "Inner City Boundaries" sounds as great as ever, but "Danger" is too heavy for my mood. "Bullies of the Block" comes across as more aggro than usual, whereas the fluffy lyricism of "Hot Potato" doesn't make me hit the skip button (I usually jump past that song). "Heavyweights" is much too much for me in this state, and "Park Bench People" starts to drag me down. I believe I am enjoying "Mary," the obligatory ode to marijuana, for the first time ever. I appreciate "Pure Thought" but shrink from "Way Cool." So I prefer the more mellow, simpler, slower material from this album when I'm under the influence of a prescribed narcotic; I guess I could have foreseen that outcome, but I certainly like this experience anyway.

 Fast-forward a week later in Earth time. I sit in front of my PC again and want to work some more on this chapter in my so-called book. I bought some over-the-counter sleep aid a few days ago, just to see what it's like, and was subsequently unimpressed with the effects. Still, I decide to try that ish again tonight. The package says to take one and to avoid alcohol consumption; so I take two and wash them down with a shot of Knob Creek and two bottles of beer. After *The Simpsons* I stare at this monitor and feel as though I took some barbiturates, although I have to imagine that this is what barbs feel like because I've never taken them, and listen to some more F.F. songs. I'm certain that I can comprehend "Seventh Seal" when I'm seeing straight; but while bent I am utterly baffled at Mikah's lyrics, overwhelmed by his flow, and jarred by the beat. I listen to several more cuts from *To Whom It May Concern* and get a sinking feeling in my heart, which is not due to disappointment with the music but because I'm piling one downer atop another and my cardiovascular system is protesting. "Jupiter's Journey," something of a slow jam on this album, recorded when the Fellowship did not truly collaborate but rather compiled solo joints and called themselves a group, is paced at a rate I can mentally process in my present condition. Jupiter was even courteous enough to insert a "three-second intermission" for fucked-up listeners like myself, who may need a moment to catch up. I put on Aceyalone's more recent solo cut "Moonlit Skies" and vaguely remember listening to it on a night last fall with the moon visible through my car windows and my mind occupied with my then-girlfriend (who was slowly revealing herself as a head case). Acey's voice takes on an added level of profundity, RJD2's drum pattern throbs but never drowns out the MC, and the chorus girl soothes my bruised brain. I determine that I must listen to Fellowship sober next, just so that I'll get it right once.

Of course, the truly sober take on Fellowship will have to wait until some other time, because it's the following day in the late afternoon and my head has been foggy all day, a state consequent to the aforementioned substance ingestion and two nights of sleep deprivation. I can barely speak a coherent sentence yet insist on adding to this segment of the book. So be it. I recline on the couch in my living room, pen and notepad in hand, and listen to *Shockadoom* again. OD's production on the first track pounds my tympanum, and my brain begins to isolate the different elements of the song. Hardly a unified field of music at the moment, this cut seems more like parallel currents of vibration. Mikah's saxophone-esque voice embarks on a brief a cappella journey. The drum pattern stomps on my head. A murky bass line lurks in the walls of my duplex home. A synth loop wails. Filtered, off-kilter keys dance on my teeth. Soon Self-Jupiter's paranoid, PCP-hallucinatory images saturate my optic nerves, connected to the brain that conducts and translates the noises emanating from my speakers. He thrashes my auditory sense with dust-inflected, second-person pokes at my bubble of consciousness, stabs through the dark of the barren room in which I sit alone with my eyes closed. I'm jumping off a skyscraper while wearing a helmet bearing explosives. Or from an airplane into a field of meat hooks. I'm about to get lynched by a crowd of angry Iraqis or shot dead by the U.S. Secret Service in front of the White House. I'd rather die for what I don't believe in.

I skip to "We Will Never..." and immerse myself in the sound waves. Not each individual element now, but the complete mix, the sum of the noises. I bathe in the warm horns—presumably a pair of saxophones, but one could be a clarinet—and feel a gentle current of bass underneath. The drums hammer at my skeleton. Strings occasionally whisper sweet nothings. And the fantastic foursome take turns channeling voices from beyond.

OK. Now I'm into *Inner City G-Riots*, the titanium standard against which West Coast indie-rap albums are judged, the mélange of moods, themes, poeti-vocal styles, and instrumental vehicles that may not be appreciated until Herman Melville has risen from his grave, until Fermat's last theorem has been solved by an illiterate six-year-old peasant from a Third World village, until politicians all speak the truth, and until suburban youths are memorizing prog-rap songs with their beverages set on coasters that had once been compact discs encoded with odes to misogyny and classism.

I wonder absently whether I'm suffering from a delirium-like fatigue. Do I really really really wanna play it cool? I don't even know who we are. After six years I think I finally understand that "Way Cool" is a facetious anti-thug polemic, unless I'm reading too much into a song that was meant only as a means to show off vocal agility. Jupiter's inscrutable opening verse involves rigor mortis and (apparently) ritual zombification, and Mikah9 depicts a creepy town without any children among its populace. Peace takes his gangster-ish boasting to graphic lengths untouched even on his morbid solo joint "Six Tray." And Aceyalone's barking vocal delivery, as far as I know, is a style he never rocks on any other song. This cut closes with the chorus, chanted in unison, "turn it around and around, my darling," which could reasonably be interpreted as the quartet's way of telling the listener that they have spoken ironically. But I'm getting ahead of myself here; I should mention for the uninitiated that this song is superficially about cannibalism, as all four emcees discuss it in unabashed fashion, from Jupiter's abstruse, Lovecraftian illustration to Mikah's macabre, Poe-like tale to Peace's matter-of-fact analogy to eating fried chicken to Acey's Wes-Craven-slasher-film conclusion. Absurd on its face—professional musicians who never claimed to be murderers talking about killing humans and eating their flesh—this track is best taken as a blatant exaggeration of the already-ridiculous spectacle of hardcore rap (the soundtrack to "cadaver capitalism," as James Best might put it[18]), entertainingly sarcastic in its parody (see also: Masta Ace's *Slaughtahouse Inc.* LP and the opening track from Black Sheep's first album) of the unconscionable exhortations to auto-genocidal violence shouted by young African-American men to their peers in cities and towns across the United States. The Fellowship is employing irony to make a sociopolitical point, and the template of violent imagery used here comes in a contemporaneous context of the trial of the serial killer and cannibal Jeffrey Dahmer and the peak period of gangbanger violence in the U.S. Chew on that for a second.

Now it's a few days later, and I'm really sober now, not technically-sober-but-virtually-drunk-with-fatigue. Pondering this little project, I realize that some readers may get the wrong idea about me or about the music I'm discussing herein. I'm not a substance abuser (I think). More importantly, I have to clarify that Freestyle Fellowship, unlike, say, the Grateful Dead, is not a group whose music makes sense only when one is wasted. My thing with F.F. is that I've listened to it so much over the last seven years that I'm searching for ways to make it sound new(ish) again; also, when I tried initially to compose this "appreciation thread" for one of my favorite groups I couldn't think of any interesting means of doing it until I got fucked-up.

---

[18] See his essay "Hiphop's Cadaver Capitalism," from *The East Bay Express*, May 5, 2003.

Anyhow, I'm playing Aceyalone's first solo album and really enjoying it, or some of it. I've had this disc since '97, which I think is sufficient time for me to conclude that this record is very uneven. I could listen to "Arhythmaticulas" and "The Greatest Show On Earth" all day—not literally, of course, but you get my point—yet I can hardly sit through the first two tracks on the album. "Deep and Wide" is a'ight, but it's followed by two (gasp!) boring cuts. "Knownots" is cool, mainly because Mikah9 shreds it; "Mic Check" is great, even anthemic, and "Headaches and Woes" is off the chain. "Makeba" is another bland song, and the album closes with a pair of so-so tracks. Huh. I cannot figure the reasoning behind Ace's selection of guest vocalists for this LP, which will celebrate its tenth birthday this year with a two-disc re-release. Mikah and Peace add value to the album, but I don't understand the necessity in putting Abstract Rude on four songs. Ab shines on "Deep and Wide"; but *All Balls Don't Bounce* probably would have benefited greatly from having a wider array of guests, which would have meant replacing him on the other three jams with, say, Volume 10, Saafir, and Spoon—after all, Riddlore, Niggafish, and Ellay Khule brought heat to the b-side banger "Feet Upon tha Table." (Insert shrug here.)

Then I bump some Mike9, which reminds me that yesterday my man Ben and I were discussing G-Unit, and I embarked on yet another rant about the non-meritocratic nature of the rap industry, concluding with the sentiment (I have to paraphrase myself as best I can) that "there's no sense in a world where Mikah9 is a starving artist while 50 Cent is a millionaire." Seriously, though. Mike is probably the most versatile vocalist ever to call himself a rapper, and he's no slouch as a lyricist, either. If 9 were six, he would probably be Curtis Mayfield, Rakim,

Prince, John Coltrane, Sly Stone, and Langston Hughes. Or maybe Amiri Baraka, Marvin Gaye, Sun Ra, Robert Johnson, Jimi Hendrix, and Posdnuos.

I borrowed a copy of the latest issue of *XXL* from Benjamin—it has an extensive article on the making of Raekwon's first album, covering everything from the choice of title to the production process—and this afternoon chose to inflict the letters page on myself. A bunch of dudes from across the country were weighing in on apparent controversies about whether 50 Cent is authentic and whether he stands among the best rappers these days. Some of the letter writers swore Fifty belonged on top-five lists, but others were candid in savaging his talent as well as his rep. I guess someone who banks on a tough-guy image probably shouldn't (or shouldn't need to) roll with a squad of private security guards. More than one pundit made the valid point that Dr. Dre and Eminem could make almost anyone a star. Several rated Jadakiss as a far superior talent, which prompted a shake of my head, right there in the break room at my job. There are (at least) a dozen emcees in the Los Angeles area alone who could not simply outshine but totally scorch both Jada and Fifty in a head-to-head comparison, and Mike Troy is one of them. I should also mention that Fat Joe was the cover model for this edition of *XXL*, which featured some quotation wherein "Joey Crack" claims the most street cred in rap, a rather ludicrous statement from someone who has probably spent more time at video shoots than in prison; furthermore, he should look up Mikah and ask what life is like on the streets as a homeless youth. In the context of such utter absurdity, I find added profundity in such Mikean utterances as "it's an American nightmare/ what you do to get your cream" and "rise and shine, my loved ones/ there's more to life than just guns" and "what makes you think you make a difference with that puny verse?" It's all love? Hardly. Some fruit won't fall far from the tree. Some fools insist on putting, in their mouths, the very last thing first . And what these bamboozled clowns fail to realize is that they are dancing on a nuclear warhead, and no one with access to the launch codes is chanting *om*.

Still unsatisfied, a week or two later, with the length and depth of this piece, I decide to try two more means of appreciating F.F. The first one has me splifted, and the second utilizes an absurd amount of caffeine.

So I watch *The Simpsons* and smoke so much of the green stuff that I can hardly hold my pen to take notes. (Of course, I had to puff enough ganja to kill my left lung just so that I could feel somewhat high, as this is "East Coast weed," as they call it in Cali, with obvious disdain.) Then I put on the "Myka Nyne" solo album; I assume that Mikah had to tweak his name for legal reasons, given the well-circulated story that he spent his entire advance from a mid-1990s record deal and delivered only three or four songs.[19] That is some intense cover art, I realize. Thoroughly weedinated, I play "Can We Smoke?" and "Hibiscus Flower," eat some cookies, and stare at the CD cover. I can't seem to focus on the music; nor can I focus on writing. I start to listen to "This

---

[19] In 2006 I would exchange some e-mails with Mikah that should clear the muddy waters of this particular urban legend. According to Mikah, "I was doing stuff then that people are doing now but wasn't doing back then, so the A and R [at Capitol Records] didn't get it. I did a nice album with about 21 songs, some of which leaked out; and others have been distributed on other LPs in my catalogue. I had my own studio, and to record songs came easy to me."

Ain't the Song," but that ish is much too aggro for my present mind state. I skip to "Life Is Hard," a reminder of the unjustifiably slept-on *American Nightmare* LP, and consider that Myka could have been as famous and respected as D'Angelo if he had played his cards right. "One Dream" and "Hidden Agenda" are on the same electro-funk wavelength, and the present listener just floats on a cloud of indo smoke pushed by a gentle vocal breeze. I must say that the Freestyle Fellowship Appreciation Project is proving much more fruitful than the Record-Film Synchronization Project. I think Mike has a cut about 'shroom use (complete with Bill Hicks sample),. but I cannot locate it and wonder if I imagined its existence. I play some selections from Acey's second solo joint, inhaling the emcee's potent songcraft and Mumbles's high-grade production . Ace in his prime was a superlative lyrismith and overlooked vocal stylist, but in my high-as-fuck mood this disc's predominantly dark imagery is a downer. Lyrics like "Ive been face-to-face with the serpent" and "the hunter likes to sneak behind you" take on an even chillier tone than usual. Sure, I better appreciate the intricate production, driving vocal style, and metaphor-based lyricism of this album with the aid of reefer, but I want something psychedelic or, at least, more humorous than Aceyalone's commentary on human mortality, governmental surveillance, and other featherweight topics. I switch to *All Balls Don't Bounce*, and the production on "All Balls" reveals itself as more intricate and jazzy than I ever noticed before. Then I make the mistake of skipping to "Arhythmaticulous," which takes on an ominous feel, given its creepy high end, rattling loop, and relentless bass line. Certain phrases, such as "everyone gets a dose of malaria and asbestos" or "everyone yelling 'save me!'/ save yourself," become newly macabre. This disc threatens to fuck up my high.

Thus I am gently nudged into sticking in the first Haiku D'Etat album—for those who didn't get the memo, this trio is essentially one half of F.F. plus Abstract Rude—which, though hardly my favorite Fellowship spinoff project, has a mellow vibe that complements my mind state. I'm almost too high to write, and I do not mean that I cannot think of anything to compose; I can barely commit the act of putting pen to paper and moving the implement around. Anyway, I now notice that this album must have involved an abundance of "live" instruments because it sounds as if, instead of sampling records, the producer(s) recorded original licks and used a sampler both to (sparingly) process and to repeat the pieces of music. I never took much notice of Mikah's verse on "Los Dangerous" until tonight; damn, that's a smooth flow. What was he saying? Instant replay. "9 in the morning," all Iceberg-referential, followed by rapid but cleanly pronounced and unusually well-projected lines. He somehow compares getting high to riding the Mothership. Much too brief. Then Aceyaloneystoneyhomey relays "it's 12 noon and I'm higher than a helium balloon," and I can relate. And, holy fuck!, Mikah's verse on the next song is even nastier.

I take a couple swigs of my store-brand Gatorade substitute and return to *Griots*. Over the crunch of Corn Nuts my ears concentrate and tune into aspects of the music I never consciously noted before. On "Everything Is Everything" I hear some low-mixed percussion that I cannot name—drum sticks against the metal edge of a snare drum? a heavily filtered cowbell?—and wonder, not for the first time, how much of my record and CD collection offers such barely audible elements. (The possibilities may boggle the mind.) "Inner City Boundaries" provides no surprises of this nature, although I pay close attention to how long Mikah and Jupiter draw out their syllables on this joint. Later I discern a vocal sample in the opening bars of "Respect Due": if one listens carefully enough, one can hear somebody rapping "keep it on like this till the break of dawn." Also, there's some sort of horn loop mixed super low during one verse, and bird-like chirps surface at the end of the song. Meanwhile the spinach is having its typical soporific consequence, exacerbated by my morning shift at work and two subsequent hours of "babysitting" duty[20], and my bed beckons.

So I reach the final round of my bout with this chapter, and on top of my daily cup of black coffee I pour one of several energy drinks available at a local convenience store. I faced an almost overwhelming variety of these beverages, but I decided to try Sobe's "Superman ™ Super Power" drink, which features taurine, L-camitine, inosital, guarana, yerba mate, and panax ginseng, any of which could be toxic for all I know about such unregulated herbal supplements (but all of which most likely have neither measurable benefit nor tangible detriment to the human body), along with a generous helping of caffeine and sugar, the ingredients I really want in an energy booster. I put on a couple of my personal mix CDs, playing the Mikah9/Prefuse73 collaboration

---

[20] In late 2005 I picked up Blockhead's instrumental album *Downtown Science* on CD, which came with a bonus DVD of trippy visual interpretations, created by film-school students, of his debut album. I watched parts of the DVD with my girlfriend's daughters, both toddlers, and attempted to answer their queries about the bizarre images on the TV screen. I eventually resorted to an honest repetition of "I don't know."

"Life/Death," the Self-Jupiter solo missions "Discouraging Quotes" and "Life Doesn't Get Any Better Than This," and Aceyalone's "I Dream" and "Believe in Yourself." To my disappointment, these cuts don't sound any different from usual: Mike's contribution to the purported subgenre known as click-hop is still virtually impossible to decipher; I still long for more records from Jupe, who should be able to get better beats than the somewhat cheesy ones he rocked for most of *Hard Hat Area*; and Ace still has one of the cleanest deliveries I've ever heard. Inexplicably, my thoughts turn to Freestyle Fellowship's apparent swan song *Temptations*, from which I once heard a few tracks before deciding not to denigrate the status I have of the group in my mind with such music, which sounds like a somnamulant creation of the quartet and certainly not like anything they would consciously record and release. In the three years or so since the album's release I have steadfastly refused to purchase or even copy it, yet I now contemplate a procurement followed by a thorough listening so that I might pontificate on its finer points, which I assume it must possess in some small quantity. Then my memory of J. Sumbi's pitiful "remixed" version of *To Whom It May Concern*, actually released (presumably with a straight face) as "version 2.0," intervenes. The mere presence of such shameless opportunism on the shelf next to the real album rubs a bit of tarnish on "version 1.0."[21] The so-called

---

[21] To this day, more than a decade after the release of Public Enemy's *Muse Sick In Our Mess Age*, I continue my silent boycott of it The single I heard was so pathetic, the video I saw so corny, and the reviews I read so brutal that I ignored the great cover and clever title and pretended the album did not really exist and thus enabled myself to maintain my reasonable admiration for the

energy drink isn't doing enough for this project, so I pound another stimulating liquid, this time Vitamin Water laced with guarana and caffeine. Ooh. Nice. Now I'm tweaking. Antsy. Scratching my arm and pacing the room. Unfortunately I'm so energized that I can hardly focus on anything, and I'm writing too quickly or else my hand cannot keep up with my head. I think I'm about to burst write out of my skin. Or split my wig, with Acey's solid solo ish *Love and Hate* as the soundtrack to my frantic act or my transcendence or my implosion or whatever it is I am undergoing. My carpal-tunnel wrist acts up again, probably aggravated by my furious scribbling, and I'm struck by two agitated and unrelated thoughts at once. First, if Ace and Jupiter can get together for a nice little ditty like "So Much Pain," why can't the entire Fellowship set aside their differences long enough to make one legitimate reunion album? (Sure, the Beatles never accomplished that in the Seventies, despite massive financial incentive, but that foursome already had restrained their internal volatility long enough to record far more songs

---

recordings created by Chuck D and his producers. Mick Jagger's admonition of "The Singer, Not the Song" notwithstanding, I choose to love the music and accept the human limitations of its practitioners. If I remember correctly, 2Mex once admonished us to "worship the music, not the man."

as a group than the Fellowship ever did.) Second, as I pop naproxen for my wrist I realize that the cumulative-stress injury in my right arm is actually starting to infringe on my life interests outside of work. This damage, of course, is a consequence of my servitude to corporate turpitude, with the extraction of profit from my labor the irresistible economic force that will not relent until it has exhausted my profit-enhancing abilities. Once upon a time in a city called Shit there lived a man who yelled "Whatthefuck?!" And he screamed from both pain and emotional distress when he realized he was stuck. So he went for help and was sent to Dr. Fuckyourself, who did nothing because he worked for the same Shitheads who had harmed the man's health. Moving right along, I understand that if the first shall be last, then I must return to Mikah9's pair of nasty, evolution-pushing 1991 variations from the norm "5 O'Clock Follies" and "Seventh Seal" and finish with his 2005 collaboration with Busdriver and 2Mex entitled "Sphinx's Coonery." I give "Seventh Seal" two listens. Oh yes, that is the stuff. (See chapter nine for my discussion of Mikah's live, slow-down, beat-free rendition of this joint.) And "Follies" still gives me a special tingle. If I didn't know better, I'd swear Mr. Troy was trying to translate the human whistle into rap-flow form at the start of the second verse. Of course, I can be expected to have a soft spot for any song that includes the sentiment "on the level the Government isn't a necessary evil/ but an accessory in the brutalities..." Michael suggests the likes of the L.A.P.D., George Bush the First, and South Africa's apartheid government are aligned with devilish elements—indeed, the "5" from the song's title seems to refer to the points of the Satanist pentagram or possibly the corners of the Pentagon—and, while I do not think he, seemingly a man more spiritual than dogmatic, more like a deist than a Christian or Muslim, means this to be taken literally, this song shares with many of David Lynch's films the idea that some element in society's power structure channels dark and destructive forces beyond human control. The passage of fourteen years has not weakened his gait, either, as "Sphinx's Coonery" attests to Mike9's continued dexterity as a vocalist and undiminished skill as a lyricist, this time boosted by a bottom-heavy composition by Paris Zax. "If infant was hiphop and womb was time," then certain rappers act as though they want to climb back into the birth canal. Mikah, for his part, has never contributed to the regressive musical products manufactured by wealthy pseudo-artists. I, for my part, have never abandoned hope that Freestyle Fellowship will reunite for one last glorious album. And thus I wait.

Chapter 6: The Annotated Indie-Rap Record Guide

One might expect me to list and briefly discuss the obscure rap songs or albums I consider the best and/or most important. But that task would certainly prove tedious and make me feel like a herb, and so I'm covering only a few dozen works and limiting my notes to a blurb for each piece of music; of course, I've shed any pretense of making this any sort of definitive discography. If everything I've heard about the shrinking attention span of the average Unisian (i.e., United States American) is true, then such brevity should prove popular. But any reader who doesn't like these decisions can and should go ahead and write the definitive annotated indie-rap discography — and feel smug about it until the book is published and moves about five units because the damn thing is so long and boring. Besides, with my guide in hand, any novice can simply skip the process of actually listening to these records, confident that he/she knows everything necessary about them and glad to have saved so much time and effort. So here it is, fresh for '93, you suckers.

Aceyalone, "The Greatest Show on Earth": grab your dicks if you love hiphop.

Aesoprock, *Appleseed*: Aesrock is great (especially when you can make out his lyrics).

Aesoprock, *Labor Days*: Ian Babbit's best effort to date, this one combines nuggets of wit, working-class anthems, and odd stories with nasty beats and loops.

Alias, "Divine Disappointment" (from two Anticon comps): if God is real, then he or she sure doesn't like us.

Alias, *The Other Side of the Looking Glass*: listening to this Lp is like watching *The Lion, The Witch and The Wardrobe* with Isaac Asimov while under the influence of ether.

Arrogant, "Fed Up" (unreleased): don't get this dude started on fake-ass rappers. He goes off on a tangent and shit.

Atmosphere, "Abusing of the Rib" (from some compilation): don't try heroin. Seriously.

Atmosphere, "Primer" (from the vinyl-only *Overcast!* EP): contrary to what one might have heard, life in the trailer park isn't always so bad.

Atmosphere, "Scapegoat" (from the *Overcast!* LP): apparently many things annoy Slug.

Azeem, "Organic Food Revolutionaries" (from *Craft Classic*): I don't wanna ruin the ending for you, but the story includes a variety of Bay Area locations.

Blackalicious, "40oz. for Breakfast" (from *Melodica*): contrary to what the Alkaholiks or the Beatnuts might have you believe, alcohol abuse will not enhance your life.

Buck65, *Man Overboard*: Buck doesn't excel at entitling his songs.

Buck65, *Vertex*: centaurs are hung like horses, and Buck wishes he were a pro athlete.

Busdriver, *Temporary Forever*: dude can rap circles around all those platinum-endowed idiots on commercial radio.

Cage, *Weatherproof*: Cage likes Stanley Kubrick films and strong drugs.

Cannibal Ox, "The F-Word": friend can be the nastiest word in the English language.

Casual, "That's How It Is": you can safely avoid the rest of this guy's output, as this is the only good song he ever put out. No, actually this one and "Oaktown."

cLOUDDEAD*, eponymous album: these fellas must be on some really good drugs, because they managed to rock a blender for one of these songs.

Company Flow, *Funcrusher Plus*: sucker MCs are wack.

Coup, The, *Genocide and Juice*: believe it or not, rappers didn't always glorify the violent hatred of one's ethnic group.

Coup, The, "Me and Jesus the Pimp in a '79 Grenada Last Night" (from *Steal This Album*): payback's hell, motherfucker, believe it.

C-Rayz Walz, *The Samurai EP*: this Bronx bomber brings everyday, real-life shit, like parenthood, police harassment, bills, and death, to the forefront of his lyrics but never bores.

Deep Puddle Dynamics, "Deep Puddle Theme" (from *The Taste of Rain...Why Kneel?*): nobody, including these guys, can tell you what this song is actually about.

Deep Puddle Dynamics, "The Candle" (see above): a candle has several parts, each of which is capable of sensory perception, analytic thought, and poetic speech.

Del the Funky Homosapien, *No Need for Alarm*: Del supposedly disses some well-known emcees and definitely establishes himself as the most cleverly lyrical misogynist in rap.

DJ Shadow, *Endtroducing*: Shadow created the instrumental record that lazy record reviewers have used as a point of comparison for eight years; other producers quietly resent this phenomenon.

Eligh, Radioinactive, and Tom Slick, "Uniforms" (unreleased): what, you've never heard of this song? Have you been living in a friggin' cave for the last decade? Is bin Laden in there with you?

El-P, "Deep Space 9mm": sometimes El-P holds his nuts with his right hand.

El-P, "Stepfather Factory": a two-parent household may not always be the best thing for the children.

Eminem, *The Slim Shady EP*: a definite flash in the pan; we haven't heard much from this MC since this self-released tape came out in '97.

Encore, "The Undercover": this is humorously delusional paranoia. The U.S. Government involved in drug trafficking? Yeah, right.

Freestyle Fellowship, *Inner City Griots*: Mikah9, Self-Jupiter, Aceyalone, and Peace fantasize about cannibalism, reflect on homelessness, and say stuff really fast.

Grand Buffet, *Sparkle Classic**: they pick up where the California Raisins left off. And they warn you that you (yes, you) are going to Hell.

Grouch, The, and Eligh, "Neglected" (from Grouch's *Success Is Destiny*): this pair is, at turns, baffled, offended, hurt, angry, and bitter from their alleged mistreatment by love interests.

Ill Bill, "How to Kill a Cop": dehumanization breeds same.

Immortal Technique, *Revolutionary Vol. 2*: the world is a fucked-up place.

J. Sumbi, "Legal Aliens" and "Sunshine Men" (from Fellowship's *To Whom It May Concern*): this perplexing emcee released, as far as I know, only two songs, both classics, and apparently decided never to compose another verse.

Juggaknots, "Clear Blue Skies": this song is so amazing lyrically that I can overlook Breeze's flat delivery.

Kirby Dominant, "Passenger 5150" (from *Rapitalism*): Bill Hicks had a bit where he tells the audience that if they think drugs are bad then they should throw all their album collections in the garbage because most musicians operate under the influence. This song is a trip.

K.M.D., *Mr. Hood*: before his rhyming partner died and he vanished for five years and re-appeared with several pseudonyms and dropped more albums than I can keep up with, Metal Face Doom was known as Zev Love X and had a great group with two classic albums, this being the slightly better one.

Kool Keith, everything he's ever put out: this is one strange character.

Labtekwon, "Nowcipher" (from *Nile Child*): the ruggedest vegan anthem ever. I love every line on this song.

Latyrx, *The Album*: next time you're discussing hiphop with some hardcore fan and he/she brings up Latyrx, of whom you've never actually heard, all you have to do to sound learned is mention that you think Lateef is pretty good but Lyrx Born is fucking incredible.

Lmno, "Hit the Fence" and "Courage" (12" single): when he doesn't get all religious and shit, this Long Beach emcee writes some excellent lyrics.

Logan Projects, *Character Assassination*: if you're having a great day and need a good pull-me-down, this disc can help.

L-Roneous, "In the Corn" (from his only album, whose title I have forgotten): I can connect L-Ron to Pantera without six degress of separation—Pantera covered Black Sabbath's "Planet Caravan," and L-Ron rocked a sample from Sabbath's original version for this Bay Area indie banger.

Lyrics Born, *Later That Day*: an affordable clinic on hiphop vocal styles.

Mikah9, *Time Table*: Jay-Z, regardless of claims otherwise, is not the best rapper alive.

Mos Def, *Black on Both Sides*: a hiphopper now over the indie boundary,

Mos dropped a solo disc on Rawkus that almost made me forget how much the Black Star project sucked. I wish he had made another one before he became a supporting actor in mediocre films.

Mr. Lif, *Emergency Rations*: this record includes a 9/11 song, an early-Nineties throwback song, and an emotive reflection on hiphop; what more do you want?

Mr. Lif, *I Phantom*: we're all doomed.

Necro, *I Need Drugs*: wholesome, family-friendly raps about narcotics, STDs, roaches, fellatio, murder, etc.

Non-Prophets, "Mainstream": Das EFX allegedly sported the Band-Aid-on-face look several years before Nelly did.

O.C., *Word...Life*: I've decided that this "slept-on phenomenon" qualifies as "indie," considering the number of units moved (not many) and the label (Wild Pitch). Now go buy a copy, you johnny-come-lately.

OD, *Beneath the Surface*: OD/Omid's 1998 production tour de force is a magnificent showcase of L.A. underground rappers. If you don't already have this shit, buy it. Yesterday.

Offwhyte, "Bow to the Scepter" (from the *Bow to the Scepter* EP): creepy synth lines and incendiary lyrics, peformed by the artist on stage while holding a scepter.

Organized Konfusion, *Organized Konfusion* & *Stress: The Extinction Agenda*: (see my explanation for O.C.) this duo's lack of commercial success, in spite of major-label connections, stands as a great testament to the reality that we do not live in a meritocracy.

Pedestrian, The, "Dead Beats, Generation Of" (from a Mush Records comp): a vision quest does not require whiskey or a hotel room.

Pip Skid, *friends4ever*: "the white race traitor" is a somewhat dorky-looking Canadian with a slightly hoarse voice and a great grasp of lyricism.

Radioinactive, "Before the Thought" (from *Pyramidi*): one of the best tracks yet from a unique lyricist (who sometimes reminds me of Lewis Carroll) using his slower flow.

Radioinactive and AntiMC, *Free Kamal*: hiphop music benefits when musicians innovate rather than emulate. How could we have known?

Ras Kass, "Remain AnonymouS": this guy can rap, I guess.

Ras Kass, *Soul On Ice*: rappers with genuine skills shouldn't squander their talent on pop-hook-happy, radio-pandering songs; also, we can learn almost every detail about Ras Kass except his dick size from this album.

Restiform Bodies, "3rd Reel Judy Garland" (from their eponymous album): this track finally answered the old question "what if we put Anticon-style raps over 1980s-synth-rock production and added an unintelligible hook?"

RJD2, *Dead Ringer* & *Since We Last Spoke*: good listening material for the next time you're reading one of your *Family Circus* collections.

Rob Sonic, *Telicatessen*: something about listening to this album while driving to work seems both fitting and unconsciously ironic.

Saafir, *Boxcar Sessions*: over ten years after this was released, few rappers have caught up with the Saucee Nomad's innovative vocal style.

Sage Francis, "Inherited Scars" (from *Personal Journals*): whatever you do, don't confuse this song with Raekwon's "Incarcerated Scarfaces."

S.A. Smash, "The Harvest" (from a Def Jux "teaser" CD): I must have listened to this song a dozen times one day, rhyming along with the catchy LL Cool J homage chorus.

Sebutones, The, *50/50*: trust no one, with the possible exception of David Lynch.

Sixtoo (A.K.A. 6.2), *The Psyche Continuum*: if the human race is wiped out by a plague caused by some caucasian-devised germ, don't say that tall mutherfucker Sixtoo didn't warn you.

Sole, "Bottle of Humans": indie hiphop, allegedly, is a demo fair.

Sole, *Selling Live Water*: like a hiphop Kenny Rogers meets Daffy Duck dressed in Karl Kani gear.

Soul Position, "I Need My Minutes" (from *Things Go Better With RJ and Al*: seriously, it takes some talent to write a good song about cell-phone etiquette.

Souls of Mischief, *93 Till Infinity*: they don't "freestyle better than Fellowship" and possibly wouldn't have existed without F.F., but this debut is off the hook anyway.

Tes, *Take Home Tes*: although not a titan among songwriters, Brooklynite Tes rocks a great Eminem-meets-Saafir flow over Beatminerz-ish beats on his debut. (Note: I lost my copy, and it's way out of print, so someone please hook up your boy.)

Themselves, "My Way out of a Paper Bag" (from the Anticon *Gigasingle*): Dose calls himself a "Nineties kind of guy" in a song released in 2001, which is really all you need to know about his sense of humor.

Themselves, *Them*: the fern fertilized in a special place by John Brown's cadaver will get revenge on humanity for its destruction of nature and promulgation of not-actually-bad rap that Dose just doesn't feel.

various artists, all of those Esoteric-vs.-Weathermen tracks (different sources): I don't really give a flying fuck about their beef, but the slew of disses these fellas exchanged in '03 and '04 featured some of the funniest material I've heard in years. And El-P ditched the humor and did a song that must have really hit Esoteric where it hurt.

Volume 10, "First Born" (from *Hiphopera*): Ten's tribute to the birth of his daughter. And you probably thought he was a tough guy to the core.

Volume 10, "Pistol-Grip Pump": Volume 10 doesn't appreciate having his style ripped off by a certain self-proclaimed "guerrilla in the mist."

Xzibit** (w/ Ras Kass and Saafir), "Plastic Surgery" (from *At the Speed of Life*): Ras Kass has an easier time getting pussy from women with low self-esteem.

Xzibit (w/ Ras Kass and Saafir), "Three Card Molly" (from *40 Days and 40 Nights*): X to the Z compares himself to Dr. Jack Kevorkian, a scorpion, and Bruce Willis, all in one verse.

A'ight, people, I'm gonna quit now because I'm getting bored with this shit and will never finish if I try to include everybody I want to. Apologies to the many artists who have made great indie or DIY records that I couldn't "riff" on. Lack of space, yada yada.

*Write your own book if you wanna object to the hiphop designation here.

**Xzibit isn't underground, of course, but he didn't blow up until after he had two overlooked albums (via Loud Records) on his belt and then hooked up with Dr. Dre; before that he wasn't exactly a household name.

Chapter Seven: Pious in the House of the Lord

If anything has helped indie rap along in its maturation it has been the unwavering dedication of so many individuals involved in the scene to their god. The guiding light of their piety has led numerous artists to the heights of creativity, with an abiding love and deep respect for the Creator and all of His chosen emissaries on Earth. These artists' devotion to spreading the good word shows in their masterful, insightful lyrics.

Indeed, it must be divine intervention that has provided so much holy insight to so many young men, the same intervention that has brought the one true God's influence to almost every human society on the planet, whether permeating every aspect of every Islamic woman's life in Afghanistan or enlightening school boards in America's heartland so that they might reject that abominal heresy known as "evolutionary theory" or acting through Mel Gibson in his struggle against the heathens in Hollywood, especially those who claim that Jews were the victims of a holocaust in Nazi Germany.

It is in this context that a sizable share of the underground's leading lights brings us some of the best lyrical righteousness since Milton was dictating *Paradise Lost* to his assistant. Though no further evidence of God's reality is necessary, we have these and other sentiments to lend us both moral support in our struggle with secularist creep and poetic flourishes for our conversations.

Whenever I meet some ignorant buffoon I can throw New England Suns member Clean Liver's rhymes "you skeptics can try all you want to fight it/ but the reality is I'll chill with the invited/ VIPs from the guest list on the day of the big show/ while y'all nash your teeth in the realm of egos" from "I'm Not a Biter, For Real." On a similar note, after a difficult day of struggle against secular humanism, I like to play the Chicago Muslim emcee Prodigal Dun's albums in my car. Monotheistic as fuck, knuckleheads: he breaks down the science and enlightens idiots and gives non-believers the opportunity to save their asses from an eternity in Hell. On a lighter note, New York's indie luminaries in the mostly secular Scansion crew sometimes insert references to a personal, loving Lord with such lines as Plutarch's "yeah, God, you know He's the man" and Wide Cadence's "I'll crush your petty maneuver/ like Yahweh punishing Judah."

The Project Blowed compilation equivalent for this scene finally arrived in late 2001, featuring fellas who were obviously more dedicated to the idea of rapping about our creator than the guys I quoted above, who mainly drop references into songs not centered on the great power looking down on us. MCs for Christ Our Savior, a semi-formal coalition of lesser-known rappers who all happen to be Christians, released an album that included cameos by two Muslims and a Jew (and was distributed by Hiphop Infinity) and entitled it *Divine Inspiration*. With production handled by the likes of Gentile, the Track Blesser, and Brimstone and cuts on several joints added by DJ Eucharist, the stellar-yet-righteous rapper-songwriter squad shines like candles on an altar. On the hardcore side of the spectrum we can hear Mysterious Ways (a Catholic), Intifada (a Muslim), and Golem (a Jew) team up for "Humanist Infidels in the Inferno," a warning to all those fools who deny the existence of God in the face of the scriptures He has seen fit to provide for our salvation. On the more compassionate tip we are offered the Prolific Presbyterian's "Jesus Loves You," which assures us that

Christ is up there in the clouds watching over us and that He will never give us any more than we can handle, up to and including death. Among the other songs are the more metaphysical "Intelligence in the Design," the speculative "If Muhammed Were Among Us" and "What Would Jesus Do?" and the conceptually brilliant "Satanic Verses."

With this compilation still getting heavy play in my CD player the following spring, I could hardly hold my excitement when I learned that Divine Cipher would headline a show in Kansas City, Kansas, and that, to sweeten the delight further, Golem, Allah U Akbar (Intifada's group), and the Protestant Prophets would all open for D.C. Providence was surely smiling on the great state of Kansas!

Though the present book had not even been conceived of yet, I did have a hiphop Web site back then, with my favorite inspirational lyrics transcribed for the benefit of fellow believers and curious non-believers alike. Alongside the sections with my favorite quotations—for example, "you know God's the man/ with a special place for his chosen fam/ who won't be crying when His son returns to the Holy Land" (Pious Pundit, "God Doesn't Play Dice") and "the universe is thousands, not billions, of years old/ disbelieve at the risk of your soul/ you can't claim ignorance when it was foretold" (Orthodox Poet, "The Essence of the Creator") and "you can't get strapped for when God comes" (Craig Mack, "When God Comes")—I had a few essays and original psalms, and this show would provide material for another nonfiction piece.

When the special day came to K.C. I, child-like with excitement, awoke an hour before my usual five am alarm and used the extra time to extend my morning purity jog by fifteen minutes and my daily Bible reading by forty-five minutes. After a long, anticipation-laden day it was showtime, and to start things off Allah U Akbar led the crowd in a call-and-response routine as devout as any the underground will ever see; half of the audience chanted "God is good!" followed by the other half chanting "God is great!" Continuing this theme, Intifada's partner Couplet Spitter launched into "The Quran Is Mad Real," his signature cut about the undeniable truth of the existence and beneficence of Allah as revealed to Muhammed. "Y'all idiots better start to believe/ the truth revolves 360 degrees/ you know it's true because the prophet said so/ and the prophet said so because it's true as the head flows," he rhymed, with some heads in the audience flowing along with him, having his lyrics memorized.

The rest of the performances were equally stunning, including such theater as the controversial Protestant Prophets member Brogue's "christening" of the front row with beer and special bonuses like Divine Cipher's unveiling of the brand-new jam "Gabriel and Lucifer."

Afterward I kicked it with all of the artists backstage, as the Jews drank wine, the Christians beer, and the Muslims tea. Golem, wearing a t-shirt emblazoned with a menorah, told me was working on a concept album based on *The Book of Exodus*. Intifada and Cipher Scripter explained their animosity toward suicide bombers. And all of the Protestant Prophets quoted dialogue from *The Simpsons*.

By far the most impressively reverant fellas were DJ Testament, Shakeseer, and the Pontificator, collectively known as Divine Cipher. DJ Testament took down one of the worst lies of secular science in one fell swoop, pointing out that everything in the room with us had a purpose, just as everything God created has one; and, despite the claims of evolutionists, God never makes mistakes. So suck it up, Darwin and

Hawking! Shakeseer reminded me that the Bible is the word of God and hence true because the word of God is true and we must never question it. Amen to that, brother! And the Pontificator said that the Eastern mysticists, the pagans, the agnostics, the atheists, and their ilk may feel smug now but will suffer greatly when Armageddon arrives. And we all concurred on the need for more punitive measures against unmarried teens who engage in consensual sexual acts—if the Lord had intended for post-pubescent humans to engage in such damnable activity, then He wouldn't have given us the institution of marriage in order to protect virtue. Surely Satan must cackle whenever two ripe youths enjoy sinful pleasures of the flesh.

But I digress, albeit slightly. My purpose here has been to introduce readers to some against-the-grain rap crews and relate my experiences with those blessed lyricists who can help alleviate any potential doubts about the omniscient, omnipresent, omnipotent, loving, and just being who looks over us from His throne in paradise before they can become actual doubts residing in my dome piece. Thanks, religious rhymers!

Chapter Octagon: The Praxis of Indie Rap in Online Postmodernist Relativity

Masai Bey, a few years back, said "how fresh I am/ rocking rhymes, not cybergear,"[22] a statement meant to denigrate "Net emcees,"[23] as though those rappers who ply their trade with modems, keyboards and mouses are somehow inferior to "traditional" emcees who use microphones and who have done nothing more than dedicate countless hours to such overrated tasks as rapping on beat, experimenting with vocal styles, memorizing lyrics, recording flawless takes, and the like, as if such things were meaningful components of a "real" emcee and as if anything can even be called "real" with a straight face by anyone who understands the nature of humans' interface with the world beyond their own minds. Bey's attitude is all too typical of those cultural imperialists and neo-luddites who value the traditional experience of becoming an MC in the "real world"—that is, the world outside the Internet—over the new paradigm wherein one masters different *tekne*[24] in different physical loci. Those who refuse to endorse and adapt to the new guidelines and the new technical disciplines necessary to become a rapper accepted in the culture will undoubtedly clacken in the rapidly burgeoning era of cyberspace hiphop. Just as drummers found themselves out of work when all rock bands permanently replaced them with drum machines in the Eighties and rock singers became passé with the advent of vocoders during the grunge period, rappers who use only recognized audio equipment, not such bleeding-edge tools as Internet

---

[22] from "Paper Mache," off *Def Jux Presents II*.

[23] a pejorative term for rhymesmiths who post their work on Web sites and do not perform vocally

[24] Greek word, often used by Heidegger, that refers to both technique and technology

message boards and chat rooms, will be left behind in the inevitable progress of artistry. Furthermore, those rap vocalists and lyricicts who thought they could improve themselves by learning such pointless nonsense as mixing, sheet music, hiphop production, and analog instruments will find they have wasted their time and energy in their quest toward a synergy that no longer exists. Meanwhile, the rappers who mastered ten-key proficiency in computer labs and bedrooms across the country, simultaneously subverting both the geographic strangehold of urban areas and the paradigmatic *tekne*, will find themselves at the forefront of the progressive hiphop avant-garde movement. Socially awkward and tone-deaf so-called "talentless hacks" from so-called "Bubblefuck" towns and small "suburban" cities (the identities of which we cannot currently name) soon will find themselves the heroes of hiphop, thanks to their forward-thinking *modus operandi*.

When the phenomenon of message-board rap battles emerged in the middle Nineties few in the Hiphop Nation recognized the contests for the amazingly transformative potential they held, though it is obvious to observers today (with the benefit of hindsight's flawless insight). A few pioneers ventured into the territory with a sort of intrepid hesitation, possibly borne of their years of social ostracism, but they blazed the paths that the truly great "Netcees" would take in subsequent years. By the late Nineties the Golden Age of online rap was in full effect, though most observers trace its end to 2001 or '02; the luminaries were shining their brightest then, with MCSkillz653, tha_board_ripper, KeyboardAssassin, maximumrhymes@aol, QWERT, ctrl+alt+delete, and MacintoshMofo all vying for the titles offered by such sites as *Caps Lock Rhyme Killer Central*, *Deaf Competition 5*, and *Data Entry Doloism*.

While the non-believers attempted to dismiss these clearly talented rhymers as nerds with an excess of spare time and a shortage of musical aptitude, the boosters and practitioners of this sweet science never faltered in their quest for total respect. As KeyBoardAssassin told me when I interviewed him, "it ain't easy to put together words that rhyme on a computer screen." Indeed, Jay-Z, Andre Benjamin, and Eminem all concurred with this sentiment when I broached the inevitable topic during their interviews, while the Gift of Gab, Talib Kweli and Slug—despite their public silence on the issue—are rumored to be concerned that their very livelihood is threatened by the rise of the "Netcee." After all, it would be counterintuitive to expect that hiphop fans will continue to listen to recordings and attend performances when they can simply read some of the greatest lyricism ever composed, for free, on the World Wide Web. MC battle champions who have struggled for years to gain and maintain their reputation in dimly-lit clubs and suchlike venues today find themselves compared unfavorably to the new generation of MCs, who need not waste their time in such a foolish pursuit as the face-to-face battle with a microphone and a beat. Juice, Adeem, Eyedea, Supernatural, and others have hung up their mics and resigned themselves to careers outside of music; they no longer wanted to confront a hiphop scene indifferent to their obsolete skills. "No one wants to come to my shows or buy my CDs anymore," Juice lamented when he and I conversed, "they just want to check to see if QWERT has posted something new on *Battle Zone 13*."

Such a fate awaits all rappers, not just the battlers, who fail to comprehend and adapt to the sea change in the art of mastering ceremonies. Meanwhile, as in any other business, individuals have emerged who have actually benefited from this logical progression. Jason Seegrabs, webmaster at *Complex Curriculum Plenitudes*, informed me via e-mail that he and Milhouse Brownitus, the owner of the site, are "channeling vast revenues and garnering respect in the Internet business community with our proactive principles of conduct" and making nice profits from banner ads, membership accounts, and t-shirts. Each of those *Complex Curriculum Plenitudes* t-shirts one sees so often in North America and the U.K. represents a small piece of the humming profit machine that Seegrabs and Brownitus have established.

Even a cursory examination of the poetry being created—channeled, really—by these unjustly denigrated lyricists reveals a richness of texture, a depth of insight into the human condition, and a deft grasp of imagery that engage the reader. Aside from the brilliant synthesis, previously assumed as impossible, of the styles of Donne and Ginsberg by QWERT, one must recognize the talent required of tha_board_ripper to pull together the disparate influences of *The Tibetan Book of the Dead*, Woody Guthrie, and feudal Japanese poetry and still maintain a clarity of vision as well as cohesion in social commentary. Of course, not all of the so-called Netcees can offer the potent prosody of Trife Reagan's "I Bring the Drama Like Maine Mall Cinemas" or the breathtaking metaphysics of MacintoshMofo's "Art Fags Can't Rap," but no significant musical or literary movement has been completely free of poseurs and fellow travelers.

The greater importance of the cultural aspects of this trend is not lost on observers, either. Godfrey Sadsack already beat the present author to the proverbial punch when he declared "the new rap is dead" and "the trifurcated hiphop era is upon us" in his already-classic piece for *Dissertation Quarterly* [25]. He is mostly correct, but he does leave unsaid the critical caveat that one should not trip over one's gamma receptor in the mad rush to crown a new musical paradigm. The scholars who usually publish their work in *The Source* and *XXL* have yet to acknowledge and bestow acclaim upon online rapping; Edward Said had nothing but contempt for the movement, even going so far as to write, literally from his deathbed, a scathing, though unfinished, essay on "the cultural

---

[25] "Triumph of the Neo-Rhymesmiths: Google, Hiphop and Plato," *Dissertation Quarterly*, spring 2004

imperialists who have hijacked the claim of hiphop innovation"[26]; Alice Walker purportedly rolls her eyes when the subject comes up.

Of course, one need not privilege the opinions proferred by these bards simply because they possess superior intellects. Post-postism dictates[27] that should the so-called nexus of praxis reveal a more intimate mode of comprehension, then the learned philosopher must reify the repercussions in the means he or she finds most conjecturally contextual. When Nas and AZ appear in a Sprite advertisement, it represents a more intimate procedural interface. When Murs and Slug dedicate an album to Christina Ricci, it represents a more intimate procedural interface. And hence when ctrl+alt+delete reconfigures the conceptions of Platonic perspectival perception and Aristotelian dualism on *Data Entry Doloism*'s "Windows XP Experience" forum, that, too, represents a more intimate procedural interface. Some may object[28] to this enclosure of gonzo phenomenology[29] and[30] "nothing"[31] within one theory, but no "Zen of microphone mechanics"[32] can overcome the inevitable dearth of manuscriptism[33]

---

[26] "Suburban Orientalists in the Rap Game," published posthumously on various Web sites

[27] as stated by Noam Chomsky in *Linguistica Phonia*

[28] for example, Christopher Hitchens's letter to the editors of *Vibe*, published in the June 2004 issue

[29] self-explanatory term coined by Kenneth Reginaldson

[30] "the new ampersand," according to Chomsky

[31] "All About Nothing," from the compendium *Yada Yada Yada: New Interpretations*, James Sadsack, ed. (New Books Press, 2003)

[32] Gun Dolo, "Versification" from his album *Going For Dolo*

that will soon follow hypertext markup language's entrance to[34] center[35] stage. And that, as Rakim once asserted, can "swing off anything, even the strings of a harp."[36]

---

[33] i.e., confrontationalism in the merging of ink and scroll

[34] i.e., toward

[35] i.e., center

[36] "My Melody"

Chapter 9: What's Wrong (And Right) With Hiphop Shows?

→OK, it's time for another non-sardonic "chapter" in this "book." And something has been bugging me for as long as I've been attending rap performances. So I'm combining the necessity of a serious chapter with the subject of a serious irritation to create this steaming pile of shit, er, this gleaming, stylized bit about my disappointment with "live shows" (I dislike that term, given the reality that no performer (not even 2Pac!) can do a "dead show") in general. Sure, underground rap can't afford Floydean visual displays or the type of elaborate background that Wu-Tang Clan had built for its 1997 tour or the stage props that Public Enemy and Cypress Hill have utilized or the expensive suspension devices that Redman and Method Man have used to fly over their audiences. And if an MC were to light his mic on fire, he might be accused of biting Jimi Hendrix's signature performance. And if anyone were to construct anything inspired by (but not ripped off from) Parliament-Funkadelic's Mothership, there would be a risk of plagiarism accusations. And by the time rap came into its own, rock, soul, jazz and various other types of music had already used a huge number of original ideas for performance enhancement, leaving DJs and MCs less opportunity for originality of their own. But come now, fellas, try *something* to make it more interesting.

→The Roots (whom I once saw at Bowdoin College in Brunswick, Maine in '97) have a history-of-rap routine, among other things, exclusive to their concerts. I saw Buck65 in San Francisco in '03, and he told a long, amusing story and then performed a song that apparently is not on any of his records; I've also seen him do his rapping-and-scratching-at-the-same-time thing, which is quite amazing. Supernatural has a freestyle routine wherein he improvises rhymes based on objects held up by audience members and a schtick in which he does uncanny impersonations of famous rappers' voices. Such unique and entertaining displays as these give fans a reason to come to shows. When a rap group takes the stage and performs its songs exactly as they sound on disc and fails to do anything other than perform without frills, we have little or no reason to attend the show, which is like listening to a version of the CD with muffled vocal tracks. I used to have a female friend from southern Cali who really likes Tori Amos and has been to numerous Tori shows, even going so far as to follow the singer's tour across several cities; she is not the only such fan, mainly because Ms. Amos plays a different set of songs for every show. It would be great if indie rap had more entertainment value in its performances, but right now the shows still lag far behind the recordings in quality.

→Now, I ain't about to start an unnecessary shitstorm by naming the artists who gave (or still give) boring shows, but a few unnamed examples would prove instructive. At the Supernatural show I attended in '01 a duo who specialize in generic, mediocre rap bored the fuck out of me, and they were the headliners; they did the hackneyed call-and-response thing ("everybody in the house say *some nonsense!*") and asked the audience members to throw their hands up. A 2002 show I attended featuring a West Coast opening act and then an East Coast duo who performed alongside a solo New Yorker had the same call-and-response bullshit, which has been a pointless staple of hiphop shows since the Seventies. Please, let the demands on the audience slide, fellas. Or else switch it up in some creative fashion, like when Sole told a crowd to reply "we live here" when he said "fuck you" to them or when Dose did something in Natti where he was a plug and the audience was an electrical outlet. Anyway, this show offered no theater or anything else to distinguish it from the numerous other shows I've been to. In 1998, at a hiphop-oriented venue in the Sucka Free city, I saw some of Cali's best rappers ever (three-fourths of a SoCal quartet and a NorCal duo), and now I can't remember much of anything about it except that I went. All they did was get up there and perform their songs the same as they are on record. In fact, the first show I caught in Cali (Berkeley, July of 1998) showcased some other underground legends, and the best performers from this collective were the ones with the weakest recordings — their energy and stage presence were amazing, allowing them to upstage their more talented but less theatrical counterparts. Even little things can help, such as when the legendary Q-Tip of iconic mainstream group A Tribe Called Quest climbed atop an amp during a performance in Lewiston, Maine, in 1996. One of my favorite emcees, who is also a renowned beatsmith, has such a long-established reputation for giving sucky shows, which are mostly hampered by his lack of breath control and his dependence on various comrades as hype men, that I have never even considered going to one of his shows.

→And, seriously, hiphop shows should start at their advertised times and include every performer who is supposed to be there. I've been to at least two shows (one in Santa Cruz in 1999, the other in Forest City in 2004) for which scheduled performers never showed (their initials are E.K. and R.S.) and a number of shows that started late.

→But enough with the negativity, because I could dis almost every rapper I've ever seen on stage, not for being wack but for failing to elevate their shows to a level where I'd rather watch the performance than drink and schmooze. Instead I'm offering some general suggestions for improvement of the overall experience. (Ozzy Osbourne has been banned at various times from various venues, cities, and states for his shows; Marilyn Manson has inspired massive campaigns to prevent its concerts from even happening in some cities; Jim Morrison was arrested for "lewd conduct" or something after a Doors concert; the F.B.I. surveilled the MC5 at some of their shows; these musicians were obviously doing something right.) Hendrix used to play the guitar with his teeth; so how about if someone raps while doing a handstand? (OK, maybe not.) Here are some other suggestions: remixes, alternate versions, and entire songs exclusive to live shows; costumes; unique positions on stage (such as a song performed with back to audience); stage props; improvisational or rehearsed skits; audience participation, but not that dumb "everybody say 'ho'" shit; artful destruction of effigies and other symbolic objects; hot chicks dancing in the background (hee hee, just kidding about this last one); and so on. I suppose I could follow with some more examples of performances that I enjoyed.

→In 1999 or 2000, at one of the many hiphop shows I attended at Rico's Loft in San Francisco (you had to go through an alley known as Minna Street to get to the door) Mikah 9, he of the famously rapid flow that too often obscures some of the best verses in hiphop's repertoire, was the headliner (or the co-headliner with Peace, I forget). He did the then-unreleased "Fruit Don't Fall Too Far From the Tree," which some of us already knew thanks to the magic of tape trading, and some of his better-known bangers, including (I think) "Park Bench People" and "5 O'Clock Follies." Then he performed the rip-roaring "Seventh Seal" twice; the first time at full speed and over the heavy drum pattern, the second time slowly and without any accompaniment. This is one of the few on-stage performances that I long for a recording of, as my briefly full understanding of the lyrics to this song greatly enhanced my appreciation of it. (In 2000 Rico's Loft was closed and transformed into office space, meaning that in the same place where a stage once stood from which Mikah, Peace, Circus, Awol, Deep Puddle Dynamics, 2Mex, Radioinactive, Sage Francis, the pedestrian, Megabusive, Subtle, Reaching Quiet, Octavious, and I, among others, performed is now a mid-level manager's office or a break room with vending machines or a Dilbert-decorated cubicle or something similar.)

→Also at Rico's Loft Anticon held a special night of "covers"; this was as much comedy as it was a display of musical talent. Alongside Circus and Awol (if I remember correctly) as fellow Geto Boys, Radioinactive got on his knees to do the diminutive Bushwick Bill's verse from "My Mind Is Playing Tricks On Me." An audience member took the stage and helped Alias when he forgot the lyrics to Digital Underground's "Humpty Dance." Sole acted thuggish for his covers of Mobb Deep and Biggie. The pedestrian reenacted that "where's my *Killer* tape?" skit from Wu-Tang's first album all by himself, changing his hat when he switched characters; he also covered the theme from *The Fresh Prince of Bel Air* as though it were a campfire horror tale. Sole attempted to do every verse from a long, wack posse cut called "H.E.A.L."—I don't remember whether he succeeded. Dose tried to replicate Erick Sermon's mush-mouth delivery for an EPMD song, with Kirby Dominant, who hosted the whole showcase in a business suit, doing LL Cool J's cameo. The funniest aspect of the whole evening was probably the fact that a writer from the *San Francisco Bay Guardian* was in the audience and incorporated his impression of the show into his article about Anticon, which is better known for its musical experimentation than for tongue-in-cheek humor.

→My old friend Cuz and I went to a DJ showcase in S.F. in 1998 or '99, with Cut Chemist and DJ Shadow as the headliners. Those guys were Cuz's musical influences at the time, and he seemed excited at the prospect of seeing them do some kind of live routine. They did, and this routine involved a super-rare Slurpee promo record, among other things, and we were pretty much blown away. (Some months later a Cut Chemist and DJ Shadow live album came out; examination of the liner notes revealed that the show they used for this disc was the same one Cuz and I had been at.)

→In my interview with Sleep he related an apocryphal fast-rap tale: "[pedestrian] played in Portland [Oregon] with me one time and said 'come on and do this song with me.' I was like 'alright.' And then I get up there and he's like 'we're gonna have a battle to see who raps the fastest.' While I'm on stage. So we battled, and we both—nobody could tell, how could you tell? It's just a bunch of [makes a machine-gun sound]." This must have been a unique spectacle for that audience.

→In 2000 I had the opportunity to attend a rap battle and performance in San Francisco in which none other than the legendary Saafir was featured; actually, this tale doesn't really include examples of commendable behavior, but the audience was certainly entertained nonetheless. After a couple of rounds of mostly-mediocre MC battles from which some chump emerged as champ, the headliner took the stage. (There's a side story here: I paid the $10 entrance fee with a $20 bill and, of course, got a $10 bill in return; the next day when I attempted to pay my toll for the Bay Bridge I was informed that the bill I had was counterfeit; I somehow managed to pass it off at a 7-11 store a few days later.) Saafir's friend Dream, a well-respected graf writer from Berkeley, had recently passed away, and some idiot in the audience yelled at Saafir "what's up with Mike Dream?" as though he wanted the rapper to comment on the loss of his homey. Saafir, for whatever reason, took the question as a diss, jumped off the stage, and got into the fan's face. Security guards held the Saucee Nomad back, and he returned to the stage, where he proceeded to talk shit for like twenty minutes about various topics, mockingly impersonate a fan who wanted him to return to his *Boxcar Sessions* style and quit the attempts to cross over, kick a lengthy freestyle about nothing in particular, and perform "Battle Drill," his signature cut. Then he bounced. This event, my only time spent in the presence of Mr. No No, was essentially in accordance with the stories I had heard about him beforehand, including his alleged dismissal of a question about old rival Casual in an interview with the rejoinder "I'll shoot that motherfucker—next question" and his purportedly intoxicated performance in Utah when he supposedly tried to battle audience members. (These tales may remind some readers of El-P's slapdown of a heckler, as seen on *Revenge of the Robots*, although my favorite moments of that DVD are Cage's sobering discussion of the stomach damage he suffered as a consequence of using synthetic mescaline and the amusing close-up footage of assorted junk strewn throughout the Def Jux studio.)

→Another entertaining act whose music is sometimes an afterthought during its shows is Grand Buffet, a duo from Pittsburgh. I've seen Lord

Grunge and Grape-a-Don four times in three cities and had the good fortune to kick it with them after a couple of shows; even off-stage they're "on," leading me to conclude that they're simply two of the funniest motherfuckers I've ever met. At the first show I knew almost nothing about Grand Buffet but was quickly convinced of their talent when they made me laugh as much as almost every stand-up comedian I'd ever heard or seen. The two dudes just got up there and improvised some hilarious shit. The next time I saw them they burned Jesus figurines, and Lord Grunge barked "Fuck you, we don't take requests" to a fan who asked for "You're On Fire," GF's best-known song. At some point in there Grand Buffet toured the USA with Sole and Sage Francis and reputedly threatened to assassinate President Bush, either on the radio or on stage (either way it's a federal offense).

→For further examples, one might look to Edan, Sage Francis, and JD Walker, who incorporate acoustic guitar ish into their sets, or to me, the bastard who desecrated a US flag on stage in Pittsburg, CA, or to MF Doom, who sometimes performs behind a metal-face mask, or to Busdriver, who improvised lyrics for an entire show (recorded and released for posterity as *Live Airplane Food*). Just give the people something solid for their money.

Chapter Ten: A Brief Story of Little Consequence

There once was a young man, deemed by the State to be vision-impaired, who also was hearing-impaired (though the State had not officially declared him so, it was obvious to all who knew him). This young man, despite his difficulties in seeing and hearing, badly wanted to become a musical artist; he persevered in an effort of many years and became a vocalist and songwriter, respected in certain circles. This was not entirely without precedent, for, a century or two beforehand, a deaf, mute, and blind woman had become a famous writer; also, many popular singers of the protagonist's day were partly or completely bereft of the ability to sing properly or to compose songs.

The main character herein had taken his auditory and visual handicaps as challenges and worked hard until he had achieved a relatively high degree of technical proficiency at his chosen craft. However, as was and would remain a common problem for so many persons with sensory impairments, his mental functions were limited—in his case, to those of an ordinary, non-artistic person.

His limitations frustrated him, and he sometimes lashed out, publicly and privately, at those vocalists and writers who possessed a clearly superior level of talent. Sometimes he ran his mouth because he recognized others' brilliance and resented them for it; other times he did so when he could not comprehend the products of minds greater than his own. The objects of his anger recognized his problems and exercised patient restraint in response to his tantrums.

The young man took refuge in a variety of pointless rituals and outlandish superstitions, comforting himself with his belief in a tangled mess of ridiculous nonsense that included purported clairvoyance and the afterlife myth. He, of course, put on airs as though his talent were actually greater than that of the contemporaries that he resented so much, but few were fooled by his facade. He eventually faded into total obscurity as a musician and spent the remainder of his life in the company of other ordinary, non-artistic persons.

Chapter 11: Scribe and Sole Exchange E-Mails Across the Atlantic Ocean, Summer 2004

A certain young man, known to his fans as Sole, and I were close friends for a time; then he got married and moved to Spain, whereas I stayed in the States. He and I shared some unique episodes in our encounters with fellow artists, but one weekend really stands out in my memory bank and should serve as a nice prelude to our e-mail dialogue.

In late 1998 or early 1999, while I was living at the so-called Anticon Mosque (also known as the Chalet or the Shack) on Lester Avenue in Oakland, Los Angeles underground luminaries 2Mex[37], Awol, and Circus stayed with us. They had a show across the Bay but weren't exactly rolling in dough and also wanted to record a song with Sole and

---

[37] Most recent among my several meetings with 2Mex was at a show he did in Maine; we discussed some subjects both musical (who from his crew was actually making a living at rap, etc.) and non-musical (family ties). He informed me that some of his partners from L.A. could not focus their lives on music because they had children to raise and thus "hiphop comes third" in importance, which turned into an almost prophetic statement for me a few months later when I got an apartment with my girlfriend and began supporting her and her two daughters.

the pedestrian at the Mosque—hence their less-than-ritzy sleeping arrangements. Sole, I must admit, was something of a slobbish housemate, and Moodswing9 and pedestro weren't much better; in short, the pad was a fucking mess, with garbage strewn throughout and the phone line cut off because Sole hadn't paid the massive bill in a couple of months. And New Hampshire battle MC Ade Em was kicking it there at the time, as he needed a place to stay for his week-long vacation in Cali.

OK, so there are actually two stories here. First, 2Mex was so disgusted with the state of the duplex unit we called home that he took one of our garbage bags and proceeded to deposit trash from the living room in it. This is the only time, as far as I can remember, that Tim/Sole was actually embarrassed that we had such a messy household. Alex/2Mex didn't bother with the kitchen sink, however, as it must have been beyond his powers of cleaning. Second, the whole fucking crew of us packed into Cuz/Moodswing's station wagon for the trip from Oakland into San Francisco for the show. You might wanna think about that for a second: the four guys who lived in that house and the four guests and—my memory gets hazy here—possibly one or two other dudes packed into a car designed to seat eight and cruised over the Bay Bridge and into downtown San Francisco. (For whatever reason, we couldn't fit the same number of dudes into this car after the show for the trip back, and I decided to make the sacrifice by staying behind; I hung out in downtown S.F. for a few hours and sketched lyrics on scrap paper until the Bay's passenger train system (BART) opened in the morning.)

Scribe: Do you think growing up in Maine made a significant difference in your development as an artist?

Sole: Yes. I was able to draw on Maine's rich Celtic tradition on old school gems such as "Hoods from the Woods" [a track from the early 1990s when he was part of a group called Northern Exposure]. All my hiphop influences after I learned about Run-DMC were very "abstract." I began trading tapes and locking myself in various rooms with music equipment until I was old enough to flee to the West Coast, where my talents would be nurtured. All the time I spent in Maine I was able to create my own definition of hiphop. I received a lot of hostility in the early '90s for being into the music; it carved me. Since then I have been able to replicate high school everywhere I have been.

Sc: Which sucked more: *The Phantom Menace* or *Attack of the Clones*?[38]

So: *Attack of the Clones*. I have grown to ignore Jar-Jar's babble and focus on his more revolutionary tactics. He clearly is a Marxist.

Sc: Do you still listen to hiphop these days?

So: These days I listen to Public Enemy hand-in-hand with folk music, and whatever else tickles my fancy. Sometimes when I need some good old rapping I throw in Eminem or Jay-Z, but not in the way I used to listen to hiphop. Listening to Eminem is like going to see the Will Smith movie *I, Robot*: I find guilty pleasures in indulging in America's supreme culture.

---

[38] This is a question I asked every data source, or "interviewee," for reasons that are no longer clear to me; I think I intended it as a humorous new Zen koan, given that that both films are equally pointless time-wasters and racist creations of an obscenely overrated filmmaker. The final tally: *Menace* 4, *Clones* 3, invalid response 2.

Sc: Who would you consider an influence on your more recent music?

So: Well, I find myself looking back to Public Enemy a lot these days, but, again, I'm mainly listening to folk music. I get my inspiration from actual events, people, and music that inspires me to speak. Ideologically, I would say I'm influenced mainly by Pedestrian... even you [Scribe] have had quite an influence on me. You were on some anti-globalization shit when I thought the world was flat. People who believe in something unattainable I find inspiring. It's tackling the impossible that I draw the most inspiration from. Lately that has been trying to speak my truths, as little effect as music can have nowadays.

Sc: Was forming your own label more a matter of artistic control or a pragmatic business decision?

So: Both. No one wanted to fuck with us, so we didn't have a choice. I don't think business and art should go so hand-in-hand. I wasted too much time drafting business plans when we should have been buying a 24 [?] and driving to Mexico.

Sc: Is there a book that should be burned in the town square?

So: Hmmm. Maybe *Society of the Spectacle* [by Guy Debord]. But only if they told people that was the book they were burning; then maybe people would become curious and read the book and become aware of our situation. Just kidding; the masses will always remain indifferent.

Sc: Name a celebrity we can all do just fine without.

So: Michael Moore. In Europe they treat him like Christ cuz he does a wonderful job making us all look stupid. The saddest thing is that he is the most visible voice for the so-called Left, and well, he may have guts, but he's a fucking idiot.

Sc: Is God good or is God great?

So: Well, Allah is grand, so even if [the Christian] God is good and great he will never be grand, so we are doomed.

Sc: Is the following statement true or false? I, Sole, would like to see Saddam Hussein and Dick Cheney in a caged death match.

So: Yes, that is very true. You could throw in the entire [Bush] Cabinet and I'm sure Saddam would take half of 'em out. He's shot people before! I'm sure he's been lifting weights in prison and will come out looking like Monster Cody.

Chapter 12: How I Learned to Stop Worrying and Listen to Cage

Like most Pink Floyd fans, I've known for years about the bizarre parallels between *The Dark Side of the Moon* and the cinematic version of *The Wizard of Oz*. I've even watched them in sync and agree that there are indeed some points throughout the course of the album that are strangely synchronized with the movie. Of course, most of the time there is no synchronicity, and most of the band members have publicly denied intentionally embarking on any such project; but the phenomenon remains baffling and intriguing . Several years ago I read an article—which I neglected to clip and save— in some publication, probably the *San Francisco Bay Guardian*, which discussed *The Dark Side of Oz* as well as, interestingly, some other examples of supposed synchronicity that included a Rush LP and *Willy Wonka and the Chocolate Factory*, though not necessarily together. Fast-forward to 2005, and the thought planted back then in my impressionable mind is taking on obsessive dimensions. Also, I cannot find the aforementioned article (I hope I didn't imagine it) anywhere on the Web, just an edition of *The Straight Dope* (a great syndicated column written by a fact machine named Cecil Adams) that debunks the whole thing. Yes, I'm aware that the arguments in its favor are contrived and selectively ignore the many moments absent any synchronicity; but the prospect of finding something similar among my rap collection has driven me to experiment a little. Furthermore (and more importantly) there may be an album out there intentionally and brilliantly (not coincidentally and sporadically) aligned with a specific movie that the public doesn't know about.

So you know damn well that I had to test some shit for myself (and the following combinations just came to me without any special methodical process, so don't bother trying to figure out where I got my ideas), and rational thinking can wait till the next chapter. I have even taken the trouble of listing the combos before the remainder of this essay so that you, my dear reader, do not have to scan through the pages to ascertain all of my ideas. Here is the list: Cage/*Dr. Strangelove*, El-P/*Blade Runner*, Gift of Gab/*2001*, C-Rayz/ *Clockers*, Cage/*They Live*, Cage/*A Clockwork Orange*, cLOUDDEAD/*Willy Wonka*, and Alias/*Alice In Wonderland*. (That's eight, a total chosen because I've been fascinated with the numbers 7 and 8 for as long as I can remember.) Among the ideas that I rejected or attempted and quickly ditched were Dälek/*Naked Lunch*, Latyrx/*Scanners* (this one did not work at all), Non-Phixion/*JFK*, Offwhyte/*Fantastic Planet*, Chief Kamache/*Dune*, Sonic Sum/ *The Conversation*, Chief Kamache/*The Terminator* and Sebutones/David Lynch.

I enjoyed some minor success at the first trial, which combined Cage's *Movies for the Blind* with Stanley Kubrick's black comedy *Dr. Strangelove (Or How I Learned to Stop Worrying and Love the Bomb)*. The first track ("Morning Drips"), which I played just as the disclaimer begins to roll down the screen, has a fittingly introductory sound that fits nicely with this prologue. And then track two starts almost exactly at the commencement of the title sequence, which is the same type of coincidental timing that helps to make Floyd/*Oz* such a disarming experience. Unfortunately, tracks three and four offer nothing noteworthy in the way of synchronicity; nor does the fifth cut, but during "Too Much" I am inspired to count the drug references in the album after this trial is complete. While "In Stoney Lodge," the next song, provides no startling coincidences, it does offer Cage's tale of his stay in a mental-health facility, which makes an excellent soundtrack to the display of absurd and irrational behavior by the bloodthirsty general and his followers, er, the men in his command, as they busily and almost unquestioningly work toward the total annihilation of themselves and everything they hold dear. Track seven is a skit, track eight is an extended stepfather-murder fantasy, and track number nine is a description of nightmares; these do not fit with the film, especially the "war room" sequence. When Cage's signature "Agent Orange" covers more of the "war room" stuff and nothing is in sync, I grow convinced that I ought to try this disc with *A Clockwork Orange*. I pull the plug on the first trial well before the end of the album. Still, I do follow through on the drug-reference tally, and the totals approximate what I had expected of *Movies for the Blind*. This CD includes, according to my best attempts at listening, deciphering, and counting, ten references to marijuana (or eight if "pepper" means something else), seven references to LSD, seven mentions of alcohol, *twenty-two* mentions of PCP, eight lines that discuss cocaine, two references to heroin, four shouts out to ether, two lyrics about ketamine (or one if "kitty" means something else), two allusions to an unidentified sedative, and one reference each to wormwood, Prozac, thorazine, and meth. Clearly, this is an album for mature listeners.

 The second experiment proved rather disappointing. El-P's ominous-sounding beats and world-weary rhymes seemed like a nice companion to *Blade Runner*'s dystopian visions, but they mixed like vegetable oil and water. I started the CD when the screen read "Los Angeles 2019" (after the title sequence and introductory text), and early on the combination held promise. The beginning, instrumental part of the first song, especially the loop, sets a nice musical background for the film's wide, establishing shots of the futuristic metropolis, but El-P's verse does not complement the imagery. The following track offers only a minor coincidence: it is entitled "Squeegee Man Shooting" and covers a scene wherein someone is shot. (Ooh, the synchronicity is amazing.) Next up, "Deep Space 9mm" makes a nice backdrop for the hectic traffic sequences in the massive, fictional city, and El's line "who owns police?" coincides with Harrison Ford's dramatic entrance to a police station; but those are hardly worth mentioning. After the length of "Tuned Mass Damper" gave me absolutely nothing to mention, I realized I was four songs deep and had achieved only frustration. "Dead Disnee" really disappointed me, as there is nary a shot of the film's urban setting to complement the chorus of "when the city burns down, I'm gonna go to Disney World." "Delorean" and "Truancy" give me nothing; or, actually, something worse than nothing because Aesoprock and El-P discuss going *back* in time. The other half of the album yielded nothing of a synchronicitous nature, and I felt as though I had just wasted my time.

   I discarded my original idea of trying a second album, probably the Cannibal Ox project but maybe Dr. Octagon or both of Sixtoo's *Psyche* albums played back-to-back, with *Blade Runner* for the sake of comparison. I'd rather not risk repeating such a useless burning of time. Instead, I went with Stanley Kubrick again, pairing the Gift of Gab's solo album (which I had forgotten about until I saw it on my "West Coast indie-rap" CD stack) with *2001*. Disappointed that I hadn't thought, until tonight, to combine the film subtitled *A Space Odyssey* with the record titled *Fourth Dimensional Rocket Ships Going Up*, I watched the opening sequences of the film with the sound on. ("Overture" is bizarre, as I cannot recall any other movie that begins with a blank screen and music for three minutes; the ape-men are cheesier than I remembered, but the monolith scene is just as amazing now as when I watched it in high school.) As soon as Kubrick cuts from the prehistoric bone to the futuristic satellite, I started Gab's CD.

"The Ride of your Life" features Gab's announcement of "fourth-dimensional rocket ships going up" and a "fly on" hook, which coincide with a dance of celestial bodies, artificial satellites and spacecraft. The second track ("Rat Race") gives the viewer one minor coincidence: during one of the refrains, the "navigating the rat race" part is synchronized with a shot of spacecraft pilots in their equivalent of a cockpit. "Way of the Light" starts, almost to the second, when the protagonist enters the film and the interior of a space colony is seen for the first time. "Stardust" mentions traveling to other planets and, in another chorus synchronicity, reflects a principal astronaut's distance from his family (already established when he is seen conversing with his daughter through a video-phone device) with the repeated phrase "when you're far from home." Although Kubrick and Arthur C. Clarke almost certainly intended to address the oft-alienating effects of modern technology in their screenplay, most touring musicians can sympathize with this cosmonaut's literal (and symbolic) distance from his loved ones, caused by the nature of his work (much like Homer's hero in *The Odyssey*, a similarity which is presumably intentional), . I can see no parallels between the fifth track and the segment of the film that it covers in this experiment, and tracks seven and eight are equally impertinent. However, the sixth song, simply titled "Up," concludes with Gab's line "dwelling in the fourth dimension, going up," and upon hearing this I realized that it hints at an overarching thematic synchronicity here. Time is generally considered the fourth dimension, and this 2004 album features some odd parallels to a 1968 flick that takes place in an imagined 2001. "Real MCs," the ninth cut, provides a humorous oddity: while, on screen, some kind of craft explores a desolate lunar terrain and encounters no life forms, part of the chorus asks "where the real MCs?/ I can't find you anywhere." Track ten is a brief, instrumental interlude, followed by "In a Minute Doe," the Gift of Gab's elegy to deceased family members, which is set against the scene where the crew of cosmonauts discover or inspect the ancient monolith. The explorers are still checking out the mysterious black slab, which apparently is an extraterrestrial catalyst for human evolution, when the song titled "Evolution" begins.

"Moonshine" starts as an astronaut jogs inside his ship. Gab speaks about cleaning up his life and touches on his battle with the bottle; such talk of self-improvement fits nicely with the image of an exercise regimen. When the chorus invokes "trying to find a way up out, moonlight..." against the backdrop of artificial satellites on a mission to Jupiter, which also has a number of natural satellites (that is, moons), I wondered whether I had found some significant synchronicity. The title of the song is an obvious double entendre, and the rapper is a recovering alcoholic; his astronomy-influenced reflections on the destructive cycle of substance addiction make an interesting counterpart to this cosmonaut's hamster-wheel-like running in a vertical circle inside the spacecraft. As this thought dawned I felt that this trial had not been a bad idea, although I could not remember why I had bothered with such a time-consuming project in the first place.

The next song features cheesy rocket sound effects and another space-exploring chorus: "buckle up and get your ride on/ I know you love to get your fly on." Then, shortly after the start of the last song on the album, wherein Gab explains that he makes music "just because it feels good," the viewer sees an astronaut in a state of relaxation on some sort of special bed with some sort of special lamp and either a TV set or a video-phone. The CD ends, appropriately, at the approximate point where the film takes an ominous turn, with the dark ascendance of HAL. So, while I clearly do not have another *Dark Side of Oz* on my hands, I have discovered some nice coincidences —maybe the Gift of Gab should consider using *2001* as a backdrop for a live show.

Some weeks later, while perusing the shelves at Videoport with the hope that something would click in my brain, I saw Spike Lee's crime drama *Clockers* and scanned my memory banks for a suitable counterpart. C-Rayz Walz had a new album out, released maybe six weeks prior, that at the time I kept in my automotive rotation; the film, like most of Spike Lee's joints, takes place in New York City, C-Rayz's home, and shares many themes, such as police surveillance, civilian thuggery, personal authenticity, and generalized urban anxiety, with the album, an excellent collection of songs entitled *Year of the Beast*. I started the CD after the depressing title sequence (a series of crime scene photos and other images of young African-American and Hispanic homicide victims). Mekhi Phifer enters the frame as C-Rayz paints a panorama of urban chaos. The only specific coincidence is the chant of "the boys in blue are back" that serves as a brief theme for the entrance of the detectives portrayed by Harvey Keitel and John Turturro, who roll through the streets in their cruiser. Track #2 kicks in just as a drug deal is consummated and a bust quickly ensues; "Revenge of the Words" really does not go well with this scene. Nas once famously rapped "somehow the rap game reminds me of the crack game," and I remembered this statement when I watched the next scene, which mostly overlapped with the fourth song from this album. Phifer's character and his mentor/manager in the crack trade ride in the latter's sedan, discussing business and observing commerce at a restaurant with a supplemental income stream; meanwhile C-Rayz tells a first-person tale about a young man who opts for the hustle, gets tangled in it, and eventually regrets at leisure from his cell. The next track commences almost exactly as the film moves to a scene inside a working-class bar, but this is where the scene/song timing breaks down, with the plot/music synchronicity following it five or ten minutes later. I could go on and describe the rest of this trial, but it seems a waste of time to copy my notes.

As any fan of both Cage and John Carpenter should have noticed by now, Agent Orange essentially lifted the cover idea for *Movies for the Blind* from the posters for *They Live*. Hence it required no great intellectual exertion to consider a pairing of this CD with this film. Hence I took the path of least mental effort. After a false start—the film starts slowly and does not match Cage's intensity for a while—I decide to start playing the album approximately one-half hour into the movie, at a white screen that helps shift the focus of the plot.

Chris Palko raps "when I first awake..." to set things off, while the homeless characters in the film cope with the morning aftermath of a police raid on their illicit encampment. Roddy Piper's character Nada checks inside a trashed house while Cage discusses the demolition of homes for thrills. This is where Nada finds the special glasses that enable him to see through the disguises of his city's alien rulers, and, like the Cage persona, he soon dares to "defy a conformist lifestyle." An auspicious start to this trial, I must say. The second track ("Escape to 88") begins just as Piper kicks in a wall and discovers the special glasses, kick-starting the real action in the film. Track number three commences almost exactly when Nada sees an alien face for the first time. Cage's lyric "if you're sleeping, you're getting woke the fuck up" actually may be an intentional reference to this film, which features a doomsday prophet in an earlier scene who intones "they live while we sleep." In an odd synchronicity, Cage rhymes "I'm walking with shoppers that look at me awkward" while Nada looks at the customers of a newsstand and a pharmacy through his special lenses; these individuals view him with obvious discomfort and suspicion. Cage also says "in the cycle of brainwash entertainment's the detergent," a fitting sentiment that comes a few minutes after Nada has learned that the mass media are transmitting subliminal propaganda to the native denizens of Earth. The next cut starts with an ironic vocal sample ("we have faith in our leaders," and so on) and includes the lyric "it's like money is god," which is not a point of view that originated with Cage (or Carpenter), but it ties nicely when one notes that dollar bills in the film come imbued with the statement "this is your god." Piper's character engages in a shootout with aliens disguised as human cops in a bank while Cage describes his typical litany of fantastic violence and advises, in the chorus, "better lay with your heat."

"Too Much" begins as Piper walks out of the bank and kidnaps a woman to facilitate his escape. The song itself doesn't match up with this sequence in the film, but the timing is, once again, uncanny. Unfortunately, this kind of sync becomes the norm for the rest of this album-movie combination, and the promise held by the coincidences from the first four tracks evaporates into the ether. Regardless, I must declare this film pathetically underappreciated.

Perhaps I should note, for the uninitiated, that Cage emerged in 1997 on the strength of a nasty but catchy 12" record (which, I believe, was released on the since-defunct label called Fondle 'em) that featured "Radiohead" on one side and "Agent Orange," the cut that probably remains the emcee's best known, even after nine years, on the other. "Agent Orange" is built on a sample from Tangerine Dream's synth-driven *A Clockwork Orange* soundtrack, a recording which provides an appropriate aural backdrop for one of the most disturbing films ever made.[39] As with my last experiment, the idea for this pairing required no great mental taxation. And that's cool, because *Movies for the Blind* + *A Clockwork Orange* = a waste of my precious time. Looking at my notes after watching the film in sync with the CD, I find nothing worth sharing with my readers.

Next on the agenda would be the Dose-Nosdam-Why? rap/downtempo project called cLOUDDEAD[40] as accompaniment for

---

[39] The most disturbing flick I have ever seen is probably *Dogville*. Seriously.

[40] Attempting to use the first cLOUDDEAD album as one half of a pair was, in fact, my friend Ben's idea. Recognition due.

Willy Wonka and the Chocolate Factory (the old-school version with Gene Wilder, son). After some contemplation I start the album as a clock in the film strikes noon and Willy Wonka makes his first appearance. The introductory overture accompanies Wilder as he makes his entrance, and then a downtempo song commences; conveniently, it ends as Wonka and the five kids and their parents enter the factory. The next song, on the same track of the CD, doesn't do much for me, although the cut ends with Dose and guest MC Illogic exchanging "jackpot" and "congratulations," certainly a nice companion phrase for the plot of this film. The movie shifts to a brief scene inside narrow, science-defying corridors and then the principals' entrance to something resembling a candy garden, each sequence coinciding with a different part of the song. An instrumental segue starts track three just as the characters look at a river of liquid chocolate, followed by creepy, down-pitch raps as the oompa loompas make their debut. The fat German kid jumps in the river and gets carried away, the freakish midgets sing their ditty, and Wonka pulls up the choco-river boat just as the track ends. This trial disintegrates during the fourth or fifth track, as the timing for the various sequences in the film and different songs coincide only slightly, and the lyrics hold no apparent sync with the imagery or plot of this flick. Still, I press on with my quest for self-aggrandizing discoveries.

And so I came to my last trial: *Alice In Wonderland* paired with Alias's debut LP, chosen because its title (*The Other Side of the Looking Glass*) resembles the title of Lewis Carroll's Alice companion piece (*Through the Looking Glass*). I decide to roll with the old Disney version, even though a more recent adaptation features a talented cast (Ben Kingsley, Miranda Richardson, *et al*) and seems aimed at older viewers. I start the

CD just as Alice breaks up her reflection in a pond, scant seconds before the White Rabbit makes his initial appearance and sets the madness in motion. The intro "Begin" has sparse lyrical content and makes a nice counterpart to the protagonist's fall through the rabbit-hole with the impossibly deep pit. "Jovial Costume" commences soon after Alice reaches bottom, and the line from its chorus that states "welcome to my world of jesters" certainly fits the movie. The melancholy and religious "Angel of Solitude" coincides with Alice's encounter with Tweedle Dee and Tweedle Dum and overlaps some of her next adventure in Wonderland; at this point I doubt I have a winner with this combination. By the middle of the next cut, my hope for redemption from the last trial in the experiment had dissolved into abject disappointment.

Hold up, though—I interviewed Alias, among others, for this book. A perusal of the transcript reveals his favorite kind of liquor is gin, a very English choice and indeed probably the same one Lewis Carroll would have made. Alias also names (fellow Anticoners) Themselves as a musical influence, and one-half of that group (DoseOne) is also one-third of cLOUDDEAD. Alias and Dose also comprised half of Deep Puddle Dynamics, along with Sole, who mentioned "Maine's rich Celtic tradition" in his interview, and Slug, who is no longer involved with the Anticon crew. These guys tour Europe, including the British Isles, on a regular basis...forget it. I'm really stretching credulity here, and it is neither funny nor insightful.

This doesn't feel fair. I had an excellent idea for this chapter, one that promised a shot at fame among college students, potheads, and college-student potheads, yet nothing worked for me. I was warned that rap records probably would not be proper for this kind of project, given their lyrical density and specificity, but I am writing a book about obscure rap artists, not my favorite Sixties and Seventies rock bands or Nineties electronica producers. Furthermore, as a less selfish motive, I can imagine great, Internet-fueled publicity for a musician like, say, Busdriver or Ill Bill if a given album were discovered as a fitting musical companion to a film like *The Wizard of Oz*. And perhaps some indie/underground hiphop head will make such a discovery, but, in the meantime, I must console myself with the immortal phrase from Donald "The Murderer of Mosul" Rumsfeld: absence of evidence is not evidence of absence.

Chapter Thirteen: The Obligatory Collection of Lists

Yep, lists have taken over the USA. The compulsive compilation and organization of facts and opinions in a roughly hierarchic manner have infiltrated the media, from music-oriented Internet message boards (as in "post your ten favorite rap songs recorded in Toronto that use a Tom Waits sample") to VH1's special programs to "laddie" and "housewife" magazines (think *Maxim* and *Cosmo*). I'm pretty sick of these pointless lists and have been for years; but it seems the more hackneyed and absurd and tiresome this phenomenon becomes the more it proliferates. Thus far no one, including me, has stepped forward to stop this madness, and that is not about to change just yet because I'm adding my own lists to the growing list of lists. I figure that if *Ego Trip* can publish an entire book of lists and somehow not suck, then I can do (at least) one chapter of lists that doesn't suck.

A Dozen Excellent Song Titles

1. "Directions to My Special Place" (Themselves) (honorable mention: "John Brown's Vaporizer")
2. "The Earl of Nine Teas Walks With Kaleidoscope Through the Streets of Yesteryear" (Radioinactive)
3. "Arhythamaticulas" (Aceyalone)
4. "Beyond Good and Non-Good" (Sole)
5. "Whiteys on the Moon" (the Sebutones)
6. "Long Live Bruce Willis" (Pip Skid with five other MCs)
7. "Poster Children for the Advancement of Something" (So-Called Artists) (honorable mention: "Interpretations of Mere Interpretation")
8. "Ballad of Worms" (Cage)

9. "Post Apocalyptic Rap Blues" (Busdriver)

10. "Fucked Up Fuck Up Blues" (The Fog)

11. "Sing It, Shitface" (Edan) (honorable mention: "Emcees Smoke Crack")

12. "Whoremonger's Singalong" (Non-Prophets)

The Four Most Popular Clinton-Era Non-Underground Rap Groups Among Middle-Class White Chicks Who Would Eventually Come To Appreciate Indie Rap

1. A Tribe Called Quest

2. The Pharcyde

3. Outkast

4. The Roots

A Grip of Clever But Unused Album Titles

1. Eponymous [Note: forget that REM used it.]

2. My/Our New Album

3. Compact Disc

4. Full-Length Recording

5. A Couple of Good Songs Plus Some Filler

6. The Mic Made Me Do It

7. Some Crap I/We Threw Together

8. An Expensive Coaster (Three Years From Now)

9. Mass-Produced Art

Six Kinda Crappy Songs on Otherwise-Fresh Albums

1. "Save Yourself" (Aesoprock, from *Labor Days*)

2. "Attention Span" (Aesoprock with Vast Aire, from *Float*)

3. "I Won't Dance" (Busdriver, from *Memoirs of the Elephant Man*)

4. "The Truth About Spontaneous Human Combustion" (Busdriver with Of Mexican Descent, from *Temporary Forever*)

5. "For No Reason" (Peace of Freestyle Fellowship, from *To Whom It May Concern*)

6. "Dr. Hellno and the Praying Mantis" (El-P and Vast Aire, from *Fantastic Damage*)

A Few Reasons Why Rappers Need to Stop Doing Those Stupid Answering Machine Interludes

1. They sound like shit.

2. They've been done umpteen times.

3. Even if no one else had ever used an answering-machine cameo on a record, Buck65 single-handedly beat the concept into the ground.

13 Annoying/Pointless Skits and Interludes

1. "A Very, Very Important Message," from Sole's *Bottle of Humans*

2. that skit on Ras Kass's first album where he and his boys discuss a woman who supposedly exchanged a sexual favor for a Jack in the Box cheesecake

3. "Westside," a somewhat misogynous monologue delivered by King Saan on Saafir's *Boxcar Sessions*

4. "Thank Youse," Del the Funky Homosapien's obligatory "outro" track on *No Need for Alarm*

5. "Blood," by Peace on Freestyle Fellowship's *Inner City Griots*

6. "A Mill," Non-Prophets, from *Hope*

7. "Leakie Leak," an answering-machine track from the Leak Bros. (Cage and Tame 1) album

8. "Interlude," from the Scribe's *Purgatory*

9. the part of Atmosphere's "God Loves Ugly" where some chick talks to her friend about whether she's waiting for Slug

10. the untitled, unlisted interlude in the middle of Edan's *Primitive Plus*

11. any of the many unnecessary interludes from Buck65's *Weirdo Magnet* or *Language Arts* or *Man Overboard*

12. DJ Pam's "scratch" track on The Coup's *Genocide and Juice*

13. the phone-call skit on *Boxcar Sessions*

Several Ugly Record and CD Covers (In No Particular Order)

1. Sole, *Salt On Everything*

2. Sole, *Fuck Art*

3. RJD2, *The Horror*

4. The Scribe, *Purgatory*

5. Necro, *I Need Drugs*

6. Freestyle Fellowship, *To Whom It May Concern*

7. Deep Puddle Dynamics, *Rain Men*

8. Buck65, *Man Overboard* (Anticon version)

9. Azeem, *Craft Classic*

[Note: a special mention goes to The Bomarr Monk's *Beats Being Broke* for its claim to having the creepiest cover I've ever seen.]

Some Fresh Songs That (As Far As Scribe Knows) Remain Unreleased

1. Eligh, Radioinactive, and Tom Slick (A.K.A. Log Cabin), "Uniforms"

2. Murs and Neo-Sapien, "Virtual Reality"

3. Dose and Buck65, "North American Adonis, Part 1" ["Part 2" may or may not have been made]

4. Dose, Sole, and the pedestrian, "Airplane"

5. Sole, "Simple Man" (he used to refer to this as "The Cult Song")

6. Buck65, "Pen Thief" (original version)

7. Almighty Arrogant, "Fed Up," "Red Rain," and "Toxic Herb"

8. Alias, "Whitesploitation Movie"

9. Ras Kass, "Core Audience" and "The Music of Business"

10. Radioinactive and Eligh, "Metrognome"

11. Blackalicious, "Changes"

Five Hiphop Artists That Astronautalis Enjoys Listening To

1. Scarface
2. Jay-Z
3. Themselves
4. Devin the Dude
5. Lord Finesse

13 Extremely Hiphop Causes of Death

1. strangulation by microphone cord
2. strangulation by headphone cord
3. electrocution by mixer
4. pop-song-induced heart failure
5. vinyl poisoning
6. seizure induced by LCD display on sampler
7. Rustoleum explosion
8. severe concussion from headspin
9. marijuana overdose
10. head trauma as a result of falling off
11. moosebumps
12. bleeding from the ear(s)
13. funky worm infestation

Eight Albums and the Drugs That Enhance The Listening Experience Thereof

1. *Waterworld* (by the Leak Brothers) and alcohol (although PCP would seem the natural counterpart)
2. *Appleseed* (Aesoprock) and codeine
3. *Circle* (Dose and Boom Bip) and ganja

4. *Temporary Forever* (Busdriver) and caffeine

5. *Vertex* (Buick65) and nitrous oxide

6. *It's All Love/ An American Nightmare* (Mikah 9) and rush

7. *Greenball* (Jel) and psylocibin

8. *Ether Teeth* (The Fog) and Vicodin

Ten Real-World Phenomena About Which Eleven Different Artists Are Passionate In One Way or Another

1. voting (Sleep)

2. veganism (Odd Nosdam)

3. a flat tax (Astronautalis)

4. Christianity (Moodswing9)

5. international courts for the prosecution of war crimes (the pedestrian)

6. the New England Patriots football team (Akrobatik, Mr. Lif, and Jacques Laroq)

7. drug addiction (Slug; hear: his comments in San Francisco during the tour DVD *Sad Clown Bad Dub 4*)

8. United States military operations in Third World countries (Bleubird)

9. Patrick Swayze (Bleubird)

10. Transformers (K-The-I?!)

Songs In Which the Lyricist Makes a List

1. "Brothaz," Mr. Lif (from *Mo' Mega*)

2. "Top Qualified," Mikah Nyne (from Haiku D'Etat's *Coup de Theatre*)

3. "8 Point Agenda," Latyrx (with Herbalizer, from the compilation *Xen Cuts*)

4. "Delorean," El-P (from *Fantastic Damage*)

5. "Slow, Cold Drops," the pedestrian (performed by Sole, from *Selling Live Water*)

6. "Mathematics," Mos Def (from *Black on Both Sides*)

Chapter Fourteen: Insert Clever Chapter Title Here

Here I sat, in front of my computer, listening to some indie-rap instrumental records, engaging in the proverbial minding of my own business, and trying to organize some of the raw data I had collected in my interviews with various rappers, when something truly unexpected occurred. My keyboard became possessed! Yes, it's true, absolutely true! I had one hand on my forehead and the other on my crotch as I pondered my next move, and suddenly the keys started to either depress themselves or follow a force I could not see. Either way the keyboard was typing some shit without any human hand touching it, and, furthermore, the clicking of the buttons seemed in line with a specific rhythm. So shocked was I at this turn of events that I did not immediately attempt to read the resultant text, but I did discern that the typing followed exactly the pattern of the beat from the Alias song playing in the background. The beats-per-minute rate of the song matched, for a few bars, the characters-per-minute rate at which my keyboard was humming along, and this incredible spectacle will remain in my memory until I'm either senile or dead. The clickety-clack of the keys and the boom-bap of the drums—meshing so well that I almost forgot that this event defied logical explanation.

I snapped out of my trance and decided I should check the monitor for intelligible text.

"keep the cd alive. euthanize the cassette."

Clearly, this text showed that the music was communicating through my computer and not that the PC was sending its own messages, although both events, at the time, seemed to have essentially equal levels of improbability. And the missive included no upper-case letters, which might have a special meaning but most likely indicated the music in question either does not know how to or does not care to use the shift key.

I hit the pause button on my CD player. The mysterious typing abruptly ceased. I pressed the play button, and the typing rapidly resumed.

"exterminate the mp3. revive the vinyl."

And that was all for that session. Apparently whatever entity wanted to tell the world something decided that the most pressing matter at hand was consumer music media. Naturally, I doubted my own sanity, as would anyone who had undergone such a drastic disruption of one's basic metaphysical assumptions. My mind was frantic. Did this mean that music was more than just an organized collection of vibrations? That it was conscious of its environment? Self-aware? Had sound recordings collectivized and morphed into a vast web of artificial intelligence? Or maybe my computer was indeed the intelligence behind the text and was trying to fool me into believing the music was responsible. No, I decided, these and other, similarly ridiculous explanations for this event were absurdly improbable, especially when I considered a fairly plausible alternative.

While I have always excelled at logic and metaphysics, this mastery of reason has always been balanced by a tendency toward occasional irrationality. Add to this equation the use and abuse of various substances, including (but not limited to) stimulants, depressants, and hallucinogens, and it is not difficult to conclude that I might have imagined that I just saw the keyboard typing a message without human interaction. I probably typed that bullshit myself and hallucinated the defying-laws-of-physics part. Or, better yet, I was still hallucinating, and no text had been composed on my PC. Maybe the machine wasn't even turned on, and I was staring at a blank screen this whole time.

I got up from my desk and walked down the hall to the bathroom, where I washed my face with cold water; or I imagined myself doing these things, at least. I returned to my desk and exclaimed "shit!" when I realized that my computer *was* on. And it *had* been blessed with a bizarre screed. Therefore this was either an ongoing hallucination or a real event, and either way I could not simply shake it off like a creepy dream. Fuck it. I would just have to play with this phenomenon a little.

I played RJD2's *Dead Ringer*, and at the first strains of "The Horror" my keyboard resumed sending letters to Microsoft Wordpad. Then I ignored the typing for a few moments to search for different genres of music to experiment with, selecting an album each to represent rock, metal, hiphop (with vocalists), soul, electronica and jazz. Pearl Jam's *Vitalogy* and System of a Down's *Toxicity* yielded nothing. While these discs were playing I stared at the sentences produced during roughly five minutes of *Dead Ringer*; this time the typing had slowed and, as far as I could discern, one character would coincide with the end of each bar. Anyway, the subject had changed.

"reform the sound sampling laws. stop extending copyright and trademark protection."

All right then. These missives addressed the legal restrictions on hiphop's creativity and then expanded their scope to the non-musical topic of the repeatedly delayed release of old creative properties to the public domain, courtesy of Congress's obedience to Disney.

I tried D'Angelo's *Voodoo*. Nothing. Dittoes for DJ Krust, Miles Davis, and Ghostface Killah. What the fuck? This whole thing made virtually no sense. Why only instrumental hiphop songs? Why these subjects and why were the messages commands? After all, the communiques could have been anything from car-repair instructions to philosophic ruminations to first-person narratives. I tried, to no avail, to get missives via Massive Attack, King Crimson, Radiohead, Megadeth, Black Flag, Fiona Apple, Outkast, Phillip Glass and the Jimi Hendrix Experience. Then I played some instrumental versions of Cannibal Ox and Nas songs. More text came up.

"the dragon with five heads and the greedy kraken and the rabid griffin will eviscerate any chosen messiah. the cult of personality cannot wrest this art from centralized control. the dissolution of the foundation in a participatory fashion must continue unabated."

Huh. Apparently the entity had read both Tim LaHaye and Ben Bagdikian and wanted to express itself in *Revelation*-esque fashion. "The dragon" must consist of the five major record labels, I figured; either Clear Channel or the commercial radio industry as a whole would be "the kraken," and Viacom would be "the griffin." I couldn't decide whether this was unintentionally funny or disturbing; anyway, what about the two-headed ogre known as *Spin* and *Rolling Stone*? It was easy to decipher the rest of this screed, once one recognized that it concerned the music biz. We could not expect an individual, an isolated organization, or a governmental agency to rescue music from the music industry, and we as artists and fans would have to maintain our efforts at eroding the concentrated power structure that controlled access to so many musical creations and performances. The Internet, indie labels, indie distributors, DIY tours, "mom and pop" shops, et cetera, would need to nurtured until there were 500 or even 5000 "major" labels and every radio station was controlled by the community it served, and so on. Anticon, essentially a worker-owned collective, and all the small, non-profit community radio stations could serve as excellent models for alternative, democratic ways of running the music industry.

And that was all. Never again did I experience such supernatural communication, and my sense of my own sanity suffered none for the lack of a rerun. I have since decided, for the sake of rationality, that I must have imagined the aspects of that day that would defy logical explanation; the essence of my accounting for the messages is that I unconsciously, possibly while under the influence of sleep, extreme fatigue or a hallucinogen, brought forth some statements of my own and later ascribed them to an ethereal entity. After all, human memory is notoriously unreliable. That's my story, and I am sticking with it.

Chapter 15: Ten ?s For Offwhyte, December 04

I had ten thoroughly-pondered (OK, hastily written) questions that I intended to ask Mr. Offwhyte. Given the circumstances of the interview and his lengthy responses, I changed the order and removed some queries. (Now, in the classic style of Donald Rumsfeld, I'm going to ask myself a leading question and answer it myself.) What were these "circumstances"? It was during the period after a performance when the crowd breaks up and last call has passed and the venue's employees obviously want to bounce. It was on the roof of the bar, with a few (possibly drunken) strangers and one friend in the background. It was outdoors on a cold-as-hell winter night in New England. It was at a time when the interviewee desperately wanted a cigarette. Hunter Thompson would not have flinched in this situation, and I didn't, either. Indeed, I liked the resulting so-called interview enough to make it one of the only two I include in their entirety rather than select tidbits from for this here book.

Offwhyte: You guys [referring to my friend Ben and me] don't smoke cigarettes, do you?

Zachary: Nah, I've never had a cigarette in my life. You're fiending, huh?

O: I was just wondering because I haven't been able to get any.

Z: All right. Well, I'm gonna start off with the last question first. What in the fuck does your name refer to?

O: This is recording right now?

Z: Yeah.

O: Well, there's a bunch of different explanations. But, basically, I was born here in the United States, I was born in Alabama. And I was the first generation born in the United States from my family; so it was some really different shit to be born in Alabama. Down there, at the time I was born—in '77—they only had two different classes of race on the birth certificate, white and black. And I'm

Filipino, but they marked me as white on the birth certificate. And I have my birth certificate at home. So ever since I found that out, "offwhite" has kinda been a term that goes along with what happened there. And also it's just a kinda funny thing that we came up with, and I liked it when we came up with it. I've been calling myself that for like eight years now.

Z: That's a pretty unique name.

O: Yeah, I just figured that—cuz I had so many different emcee names and they were all wack. And when I came up with Offwhyte I was chilling with my friends, and we were making up a gang called the Whitestones. In Chicago, there's a really notorious gang called the Blackstones. And they're for real. And we were making up the Whitestones just for fucking around, you know. And naming each other, everyone had to have a name that pertained to white. So then I was Offwhyte. And they were saying that I should really, seriously *be* Offwhyte. And that was better than all the other names that I had come up with, so it became my moniker after that.

Z: I'm documenting hiphop history here.

O: [Laughs] And the birth certificate thing was real, too.

Z: What month was you born in?

O: August, August 22nd.

Z: Huh, I was born on September 6th that year.

O: Oh, you're a Virgo. I'm a Leo, but I'm right at the cusp of Virgo.

Z: There was a bunch of us [indie rappers] born right around then. Either Lord Grunge or Grape-a-Don was born in the middle of that September. Sole, pedestrian, et cetera. Who would you have elected, Satan or Satan?

O: Satan or Satan? I don't know, man. I voted for Kerry, but the only reason I voted for Kerry is because Bush is getting away with a lot of different shit. First of all, there is a war going on that doesn't necessarily need to be as drawn out as it has been. Just been fucking shit up over there since the get-go. But other than that everything you hear abut Bush is just negative, man. I mean, he's doing some really bad things for the environment. One of my best friends is Native American, and he [Bush] has lifted a lot of the laws that pertain to protecting Native American culture and land.

Z: So it's OK to dump nuclear waste in a Navajo burial ground.

O: Yeah, he's dumping shit on their land, and he's getting away with it!

Z: Right, and he controls the Government, so---

O: The shit is just fucked up, man. I voted for Kerry, not necessarily because I'm a Democrat or because I thought he was the best candidate or whatever. But, on the real, these are some really fucked up times, and President Bush has contributed to making this a fucked up time. And I was not happy with the outcome of the election at all. Most cats I knew weren't.

Z: Well, there's a Nas line where he says, "who you gonna elect, Satan or Satan?"; and Kerry's pretty bad, that's why I—

O: It's gonna take a long time for real change to come around, unfortunately. Doing the things we do, like traveling around to different places and performing, really puts us in touch with a lot of cats that are still on the level, that still appreciate what reality has to say; and that's what we appreciate the most.

Z: Which was wacker, *The Phantom Menace* or *Attack of the Clones*?

O: You know what, *Attack of the Clones* was a'ight, simply because it had more action in it. The special effects were definitely stepped up. *Phantom Menace* was completely wack because it had Jar Jar Binks and stuff. That shit was mad annoying.

[At this point a local DJ-producer breaks in and talks for a minute with Offwhyte, who also tries to score a cigarette from a tipsy guy nearby.]

Z: Would you rather have your vote get deleted in a computer or get thrown out by hand?

O: Damn, thrown out by hand because when I went to vote—in Illinois we still use paper, and I'd rather have it be on paper because at some point that one vote that I cast was in existence.

Z: How do you think Barak Obama would respond if Alan Keyes walked up on him and punched him in his grill?

O: He would probably offer a politically correct speech that would enable—

Z: Not bust him back?

O: No, man, I don't think he would bust him back.

Z: You're from Illinois. I don't really know him that well.

O: It's interesting you would bring that up because the Obama/Keyes thing has been really big this year, obviously, with the election. Everyone loves Obama. And I don't have a problem with Obama. He's cool, and I think he can go a good job. But, man, people are just on his jock, hardcore. The fact of the matter is, of someone clocked him, I don't think he would clock him back. I think he would try to stay as politically correct as possible.

Z: True or false? Donovan McNabb deserves the NFL's MVP award this year.

[Some guy in the background says "false" and tries to say something about McNabb's mythical inability to win games for his team.]

O: Uh, false. I'm gonna have to go with what ths guy said.

Z: Why is the new Eminem album so crappy?

O: Honestly, dude, I haven't heard it. I heard the single ["Mosh"], and I have it [the album] downloaded at home; I just haven't burned a disc for myself. [Note: the rumor is that Slim Shady threw together a wack LP in response to the early leakage of what would have been his album.]

Z: Alright, one last question. On the only planet revolving around the fifth sun, does the merchant of complex destiny have reincarnated gonads?

O: [Laughs at Scribe's clever combination of song titles.] Yes. And shouts out to all the good people of Portland. You make us feel very comfortable.

Chapter Sickteen: Styling

"To my mind, *technique* is inseparable from what is finally played as content."
(LeRoi Jones, "The Jazz Avante-Garde," 1961)
"I can sneeze, sniffle, or cough/ e-e-even if I stutter I'll still come off"
(Big Daddy Kane, "Set It Off," 1988)

I originally wanted to write a chapter devoted exclusively to "fast" rapping, until I realized the difficulties inherent in such an endeavor; that is, how to determine what might constitute fast rap, whether a cadence was rapid or just unique, *et cetera*, not to mention the unnecessary limitation to speed as a criterion. Thus I decided to write a piece about vocal styling in general, by which I mean rapping in a manner other than the same old straightforward mode *and* switching it up for different songs. Not rocking one style, no matter how distinct or spectacular, is an important element of styling, of course, and only a relative smattering of rappers—although some of the best (or, at least, my favorite) MCs have ignored this skill—have proven themselves capable.[41] My fondness for

---

[41] I should note that a few household-name rappers, namely Andre Benjamin, Jay-Z, Biggie, Nas, and Eminem, have demonstrated an ability to really flip some other shit, but these guys hardly need any publicity at this point.

the music of mic controllers as diverse as Bigg Jus, Sixtoo, MF Doom, and Rob Sonic, on the indie circuit, or Rakim, Scarface, Common Sense and Chuck D, from the major labels, aside, I must admit that they and many others sound virtually the same from one song to the next. The rapper-songwriter types who choose to vary both their delivery and their lyrical content[42] over the course of an album or a show deserve special recognition, since their efforts have aided the progress of rap's artistry as much as creative production and challenging lyricism have.

Sometimes it seems as if some viral meme has spread quietly through the continental United States. It takes a vaccine cocktail derived from ignorance, tone deafness and myopia to inoculate a listener exposed to the evolved strains of rap vocalism. And the contagion requires little more than an accumulation of spit and an exhalation of breath, expelled by twisted vocal cords through sneering lips, to proliferate.

---

[42] For example, the normally hyperkinetic Riddlore slows his roll for the satirical "How to Make It Big in the Record Industry" (from his DIY CD *Everything You Need to Know...*), achieving a sluggish-thuggish pace that enhances his mockery of rap-by-numbers hardcore MCs.

Cough. One early vector of the disease is known as Pharoahe Monch. His baritone seems to bellow down from some fog-enshrouded mountaintop, though he would more likely be found perched on the smog-choked upper levels of a Queens apartment building. This griot enunciates so cleanly that the trained ear can find few words in his body of work left open to debate among, say, splifted Organized Konfusion fans; each crisp syllable is like one molecule among the released hypnotical gasses. And sometimes Pharoahe likes to drrrag out ppparts of his pppolysyllabic havoc before he ejaculates poetical perception. If underground-rap aficionadoes were more superstitious, then Pharoahe's massive talent might have inspired an urban legend of the Robert Johnson persuasion, something of Faustian equivalence that befits his seminal influence.

Cough. DoseOne floats over the beat like a fluffy cloud on a sunny August afternoon. An accumulation of cumulus during a dry month in the East. He rumbles, on occasion (see: parts of *Circle*), kinda like a Harley-Davidson in a densely populated neighborhood. Maybe there's a bird trapped in his throat, and avian melodies soar from his windpipe whenever he opens his mouth and allows the creature to express his or her birdly poetic observations for the enjoyment of the enlightened world. If great poetry is beauty in the unconcealment of truth, and if Dose is a talented poet with a scat-singer animal in his throat, then his rapistry is poetry vociferated by a primal melody. The spotted warbler? The North American scale finch?

Cough. When K-The-I's voice hits the mic, he electrocutes spit. His saliva is sprayed into the device and produces brilliant sparks. And, incredibly enough, they fail to touch and sterilize the viral strain that has infected his mouthpiece. It booms and bounces with impunity, delivering messages both personal and societal via infectious moisture from his membranes. Kiki may not have three million robots to command, but billions of his brain cells infected with the plague of rhymerculosis have induced paroxysms of rapid-fire vocal projection.

Cough. In the DJ/turntablist documentary film *Scratch* a dude at some kind of DJ school displays his musical notation for different scratches, eliciting disbelief in at least one viewer. Whatthefuck? Howthefuck? Such a move represents either the triumph of an excessively logical mindset in art or the integration of left-brain principles with the human creative faculty. But hold up...how might that concept apply to the vocal element of hiphop music? It is not as ridiculous as it may seem initially, considering that musical notation has long been applied to singing, as well as, in a somewhat primitive form, percussion. And rapping may be seen as a percussive style of singing or a percussion-driven oral poetry. So it's not so far-fetched. Still, an approach similar to music theory may prove ineffective without the inclusion of an ad hoc prosody specific to rap. The chameleonic Gift of Gab could prove an interesting test subject. He has one thing where he extends one part of a word, which may not even be an entire syllable, just enough to accentuate a sentiment, usually at the end of a line, and then replicates it at the end of the subsequent line. The unsilent partner in Blackalicious has another thing where he unleashes a staccato barrage of words, which might be graphically represented as something like the fluctuations of the Dow Jones average on any given day. Additionally, Gab has at least one joint (the one-verse, no-chorus "Rhymes for the Deaf, Dumb, and Blind," from *Melodica*) wherein he places his rhyme about one second before the beat hits for long stretches of bars and at least one cut ("Attica Black," from *Melodica*) wherein he seems to be vociferating from somewhere deep in his esophagus. No, I do not think that anyone can chart the fluctuations and notarize the intonations and enumerate the cadence of one emcee, let alone all of them. Should some foolhardy musicologist attempt such a feat, he or she most likely would develop a futile obsession, at best, or a non-contagious mental illness, at worst.

Cough. I've seen Peace up close several times and have never noticed any indication of bubonic plague. Nor did his skin show signs of flesh-eating bacteria. Nor were his eyes jaundiced. If he were to have an MRI done of his head, I doubt his brain would appear spongy. The infection must be in his lungs. The rasp-edged bass that emerges from his throat also makes him sound a bit like a man who has quenched his cotton-mouth with a steaming yerba mate drink. At his best, Peace has delivered an almost trance-inducing flow, from "Physical Form" (off Freestyle Fellowship's first album) on up to "Ego Sonic War Drums" (his recent collaboration with Blackalicious). If he were to take his lyrics in a mystical or psychedelic direction, his combination of voice, cadence, and projection would make him resemble a shamanic emcee or a modern counterpart to the likes of Arthur Rimbaud and William Blake.[43] Perhaps he should

---

[43] Jonathan Franzen, in his collection of essays *How To Be Alone*, states that

be tested for synesthesia.

Cough. Radioinactive has chops. Oh, yes. When he wants to show off, he can get as choppy as Ernest Hemingway's prose. Think guillotine. Think lumberjacks in a redwood forest. Think old Ginzu knife commercials. He can chop a beat lengthwise or edgewise. Chopping it up so easily, Radio' doesn't need MTV or PCP. Just pair him with AntiMC and let them be. One might wonder if Kamal froths at the mouth in the recording booth, rapidly rapping like a rabid madman and hacking up beats with an ax-esque tongue.

Cough. Lest anyone forget that every chop is preceded by a swing, Freestyle Fellowship (with "Hot," off the first Project Blowed compilation, and the original version of "Danger," included on Mikah's *Time Table*) and the Oregonian trio Lifesavas (for "State of the World," off *Spirit in Stone*) offer a modernized rap-centric primer on jazz vocalese that even Annie Ross might appreciate. Ahem.

"today's Baudelaires are hiphop artists."

Chapter 17: Mandrake and Me

"This is my ego trip/ you weren't invited" (Mandrake, "DAT Damage")

In his subculture he is a legend, an autodidact of near-mythic stature enshrouded in tales that have lifted his mystique beyond the reach of the man himself. Like Vincent van Gogh, Sun Ra, and Hunter Thompson, his persona is probably as responsible for his appeal as his art, and he certainly rivals those three and most others of their ilk in the field of eccentricity. The verifiable pieces of his legend often contribute a feel of plausibility to even some of the most outlandish stories about the emcee known as Mandrake. And, oh yes, he eludes interviews. The present author exchanged e-mails with Mandrake for two weeks before finally securing a phone conversation—I would call him at a certain time at a number he claimed was connected to a pay phone—that I hoped would clear some of the fog obscuring the man.

He refused to reveal his government name and age but offered his birthday (August 8th) and birthplace (Philadelphia). Not satisfied with this chat via fiber-optic cables, I tried to lull him into a state of suggestibility that might help convince him to agree to a face-to-face meeting. So I started lobbing softball questions at him. His favorite rapper? Pharoahe Monch. Did he really prefer psych- and prog-rock to rap these days? No, but he listens to bands like The Soft Machine and Atomic Rooster frequently. Digital or analog recording? "A mixture of both." Then I tried to slip in "how about an in-person interview?" I'm lucky he didn't simply cut off the convo right then.

"If you ask me that again," he responded, "I will hang up this phone."

I apologized, though one can hardly blame me for attempting to meet a man who, apparently, had not been the subject of a clear photograph since his middle school days, a rapper who had given his fans just twelve live performances, all of which involved some means of obscuring his face, during a ten-year career. Still, I managed to pump a few good responses out of him during the seven minutes he deigned to speak with me.

A much-repeated part of his legend holds that, sometime during the Nineties, Mandrake, driven to achieve a unique sound for his drum loops, once pulled the magnetic tape from a cassette, covered the recording material with Scotch tape, re-wound the tape around the spools, and used the resulting cassette contraption as a primitive filter for his programmed beats.

"That story is semi-true," he told me. He used that device for only the snares on only one song, specifically his homage to Schooly D ("Looking at My Timex").

How about the rumors of jail time for statutory rape?

"Definitely bullshit. Several years ago the cops showed up at my old apartment to investigate allegations that I had an underage girl there with me. But the chick was eighteen, not fifteen, and showed them her ID and shit. Turned out her parents had lied to the police because they didn't like me."

I inquired whether "Clown School" is, as purported, directed at Ikon from Jedi Mind Tricks. His reply was both curt and negative. "You brain stems are accomplices in no accomplishments/ star geeks who plagiarize ideas but don't acknowledge it"? This track is a just-vague-enough diss, practically standard for rappers.

Another rumor has him writing his entire 80-minute magnum opus (entitled *Magnum Opus*) during a two-day Addirol bender. But he informed me that he has never used "that high school kid shit" and actually composed the lyrics to that album under the influence of middle-shelf vodka.

Then he added, without prompting from me, a comment that I can only assume was a joke.

"I always write my songs in a code used the Allies during World War II, transfer them to my PC, save them in a restricted-access folder, and shred the original drafts. I don't want anyone biting my lyrics before I can record them."

He replied "no comment" to my queries about whether he had been inspired by rubber-cement fumes to write "The Hypocritical Oath," if he truly penned the second verse from "Technical Foul" while asleep, and how he invented the verb-free chorus.

Grasping for almost anything, I then asked him why he was reclusive.

"Because it keeps you all guessing," he said.

There was a pause in the dialogue, and I opened my mouth to speak but stopped when I realized I would be conversing with the dial tone. Fuck. That bastard has great timing.

Among the Mandrake yarns I had no opportunity to question him on, the more plausible ones: he had memorized the entire "X" section of *The American Heritage Dictionary* (either in the fifth grade or in county jail or during the night shift at a hotel job); he is fluent in Farsi; someone once stabbed him in a supermarket parking lot; he owns a complete DVD collection of the films, including the really crappy ones, of Rosario Dawson (whom he considers the most beautiful woman he has ever seen); and he once engaged in fisticuffs with Kanye West over religion, royalties, a white chick, or musical plagiarism. Also, depending on who is claiming insider info, 'Drake suffers from any of several mental illnesses. On this he has been dodgy, essentially admitting to a disorder but obscuring its exact nature. E.g., he thanks Paxil, lithium, marijuana, whisky, *and* Klonopin in the CD booklet from *Brain Cleaner*. E.g., he states "I don't feel repressed/ I repress my feelings" on "The Ministry of Love."

I do not know what to make of most of the urban legends surrounding this guy, but they undoubtedly make Mandrake more than a mere artist or entertainer; he is elevated to a sort of one-man phenomenon. When Billy Corgan sued 'Drake over an uncleared Smashing Pumpkins sample—and it was obvious that the bit in question was borrowed from "Bullet With Butterfly Wings" —there seemed little doubt that Corgan would prevail in court. Humorously, the initial articles in publications like *The Source, Spin,* and *Billboard* could offer neither a photograph nor the legal name of the defendant in the case. The follow-up pieces, some of them published in daily newspapers as curiousities, that appeared in the following weeks revealed a lawsuit that dissolved when the defendant could not be located or definitely named. Penal Colony Music, Mandrake's supposed ASCAP affiliate, was exposed as fictitious, and Thermodynamic Recordings,. his record label, turned out to consist of nothing more than an offshore bank account and a Brooklyn P.O. box rented to someone who used a phony ID and the name Holden Pilgrim. Corgan's legal representatives were forced to take action against Mandrake's North American distributor, who pulled all unsold copies of the album in question (*Cantos*) and settled out of court for an undisclosed sum.

I imagine that if Mandrake ever emerges from his secret identity or underground bunker, he will do so in a grand fashion befitting his stature. Some stunt inspired by both David Blaine and Michael Moore, something in the vein of levitating the Pentagon or, better yet, an activity borrowed from Project Mayhem would properly cement his legend.

Chapter Eighteen: But Seriously, Folks

"In the old wars kings quarreling and thousands of men following.
In the new wars kings quarreling and millions of men following.
In the wars to come kings kicked under the dust and millions of men following great causes not yet dreamed out in the heads of men." (Carl Sandburg, "Wars," c. 1916)

I realize that some readers at this point may be wondering where Mr. Fuck the GOP has gone; like, why have I been so deadly non-serious and apolitical for so much of this book thus far? The answer is simple. I usually haven't felt like writing anything smart and serious, and no one is paying me to do this ish so I'll write whatever I damn well feel like writing. This is my PC, and it will serve my nefariously humorous purposes if I so desire. In the words of that renowned existentialist Casual, "get the fuck off my dick and let me rip this shit" (from "That's How It Is"). So enough of this stand-up comedy bullshit. This chapter is gonna be scholarly and shit.

The natural human impulse against authority is quite strong, though almost entirely beaten out of us by adulthood. Remnants of this bent remain, of course, throughout the typical lifespan, and sentiments of this nature can find expression in places as varied and unexpected as graffiti-enhanced subway tunnels, big-budget motion pictures, and obscure rap songs. Of course, anarchism or libertarian socialism or whatever you might want to call it has hardly taken underground rap by storm, and, in fact, religious sentiments may even outnumber anti-authoritarian sentiments in indie-rap lyrics (though not as overwhelmingly as in the mainstream, where God gets more credit in liner notes than, say, Bakunin or the Black Panthers). Still, the stubborn insistence by a minority element on occasionally dismissing capitalism, the State, religion, or any of the other major systems of authority reassures me that humankind hasn't completely accepted defeat at the hands of its rulers. Yet. Oh, and I suppose a disclaimer is in order: no, I don't think lyrical content should be devoted exclusively to social commentary—anyone who's subjected him/herself to the length of any of my CDs can attest to the examples I have set for topical variety, not to mention my variety of personal choices in listening material.

First off, the Coup is too obvious for my purposes. Boots Riley is a great MC and a dedicated activist, and I think the records he and his supporting cast released during the Nineties are inspiring and off the chain and so on, but his criticism of the Powers That Be, like that of Chuck D, dominates his lyrics so thoroughly that I can find little intellectual challenge in locating and discussing them for this piece. The same goes for the up-and-coming Nate Mezmer, whose debut *Kill the Precedent* excludes social commentary from only one song, by my count (specifically his caustic send-off to an ex-girlfriend).

Other poetically radical thought finds occasional expression in lines or verses from the likes of DoseOne, Lmno, Mikah 9, Ill Bill, Mr. Lif, Immortal Technique, Busdriver, Sage Francis, and Aesoprock. (At this point some readers who either have never heard of these guys or have not listened closely to their statements may feel incredulous, but they (especially) should bear with the author.) In the skyscraper that is the collected works of these rappers, rejection of essential socio-political systems might comprise one floor or less, but that fraction is no less important for its relative tinyness.

While this essay can make no pretense of assembling either a coherent shared narrative or a general rejection of authority in the canons of these songwriters, it can offer insight into the bits of anarchistic wisdom that they channel for all-too-brief bars of music. The earliest example one will find from any of these dudes is Mikah's blistering "5 O'Clock Follies," one of his two solo contributions to Freestyle Fellowship's seminal debut album in 1991. If one can somehow ignore the virtuosic vocal performance that the former Microphone Mike delivers for this joint and instead concentrate on the lyrics—as difficult as they are to decipher at times—a clearly anarchic thrust, perhaps borne of the man's experiences with dire poverty, reveals itself. The segment where Mike Troy asserts "on a level the Government isn't a necessary evil/ but an accessory in the brutalities of the mercenaries of the modern-day Sodom and Gomorrah horror" dismisses the common response to arguments against government (as well as imprisonment and warfare, among other things) that one might call the Doctrine of Necessary Evil. Mikah's juxtaposition here of governmental brutality with the infamous myth of Sodom and Gomorrah, which has been used as an excuse for the Christian repression of sexual freedom for many centuries, is intriguing. The monotheistic deity shared by Christianity, Islam, and Judaism, of course, serves both as a model and as a rationale for hierarchy and as a supernatural bogeyman who will exact punishment on those who cross "His" chosen rulers. The fictional peoples of Sodom and Gomorrah had the gall to disobey the fictional deity's (and, by extension, the factual social elite's) absurd regulations of sexual behavior and thus suffered the greatest earthly penalty imaginable, a scenario not dissimilar from the fate of those who would disobey the medieval Catholic Church or the modern White House. Elsewhere, amid references to COINTELPRO, colonialism, and prison, the musician disavows any identity as a militant but proclaims there remains a part of him that "don't give a fuck." Then he launches into "fuck Bush, fuck Quayle, and the whole Republican crew/ and the Democratic, get the automatic [firearm]/ I've had it with the Red, White, and Blue/ and dos and don'ts, I'm breaking all the rules"; this establishes a clear and non-partisan disdain for the so-called rule of law. Nuff said.

So who else harbors a little healthy animosity toward authority? Certainly Circus, of Los Angeles underground crew the Shapeshifters, who, among all of his bizarre talk about space aliens and Freemasons, drops the distinctly anti-capitalist nugget "the invention of money/ a machine, murdering" on the posse cut "Holy Shit!" (from Anticon's first two compilations). And Aesoprock seems to understand capitalism, or, at least, labor for money, as a system wherein "the slaves work for assholes/ and the assholes work for kings" (from "Kill 'em All," on a Def Jux compilation) as well as the common human struggle within a socio-economic structure that they cannot control ("all I ever wanted was to pick apart the day/ put the pieces back together my way," from "Daylight" on *Labor Days*—although this may be a misinterpretation). Busdriver (who titled his DIY debut *This Machine Kills Fascists*) apparently recognizes Christianity for the distraction that it is: "our situation ain't improving with a Bible" (part of the chorus on "Driving Under the Influence," from *Memoirs of an Elephant Man*). Futhermore, "claiming ownership of this Pangea puzzle piece [North America] is *so* English settler," according to Busdriver's *Temporary Forever*. And Ill Bill of New York's Non-Phixion knows the time. On "American History X" he says what most of us already realize, though we may not state it aloud: "whether Democrat or Republican/ same scum-bag government/ with the same scum-bag ways of running shit." On his older solo track

"How to Kill a Cop" (modeled after Redman's "How to Roll a Blunt") Bill, presumably unaware of the common anarchist description of police officers as goons for the upper class, nevertheless parallels this conception with the two lines "then you realize what police is/ government-funded gangbanging thugs." Meanwhile the elusive Canadian called Knowself—the rumors I've heard about this guy could constitute a chapter of their own—dropped the following (clearly anti-capitalist) gem on Pip Skid's posse cut "Long Live Bruce Willis": "there's no such thing as private property/ no land is yours." (Yes, I realize that this paragraph is running quite long; if you don't like how I handle my biz, read DMX's memoirs or an Al Franken tract or something.) Priest, of the defunct Anti-Pop Consortium, says, "fuck a president/ nominate peace for dictator" on "Disorientation"; Ras Kass describes capitalism as "the socio-economic guillotine" in "Reelishymn." Aceyalone, another member of Freestyle Fellowship, strikes an almost-paranoid note with his dark, Orwellian statement on that covert means of repression known as surveillance; "The Walls and the Windows" (from the amazing LP *A Book of Human Language*) features the chorus "the walls have ears/ the windows have eyes/ and a dead man tells no lies." Sage Francis, who normally shies from specific social commentary and opts instead to create such politically less substantive but rhetorically more visceral songs as "Makeshift Patriot" and "Mourning Aftermath" (both in response to the 9-11-01 situation), also goes the Orwellian (or Floydean) route with the essay-like "Majority Rule," a b-side cut. Apparently recognizing the indoctrinating nature of the U.S. educational system and its role in maintaining the social superstructure, Sage instructs "whatever you want the truth to be/ simply fool the masses/...get them in elementary school and college classes/ eventually you'll rule their cowardly asses." There probably hasn't been this much of an Orwell influence in music since the Seventies (see David Bowie's *Diamond Dogs* or Pink Floyd's *The Wall*).

Speaking of the educational system...DoseOne's lyrics to "Eating Homework," one of twelve songs that comprise the hiphop album that is among the absolute best and possibly is *the* best ever (*Them* by Themselves, the duo in which Dose is the rapper and Jel the sampler technician), reject the aims and methods of mass schooling. The man who attended the University of Cincinnati as Adam Drucker laments, with some bitterness, "my formative years were spent/ projecting myself out that window/ from the chair with the desk/ bolted to it, bolted to it," thereby both attacking the loss of irreplacable childhood time with classroom confinement and, less obviously, comparing the elementary-school student to a manufactured object (that is, the desk and chair are literally bolted together while the kid is figuratively restrained by the furniture). This is especially relevant when one reflects that the public-school system and its general norms of operation were designed mostly to train working-class children for factory work. Dose also takes a humorous jab at his time spent in school: "so I wonder/ has my doodling suffered?" Indeed, when the boy who would grow to become a musician, poet, and entrepreneur was being compelled to memorize and "take note of as precious" everything "from the Pledge of Allegiance on down to the correct spelling of *success*" — while these may be random examples of the sort of trivia that schools typically belabor, Drucker more likely chose them for their symbolic boost — the imagination that would prove so valuable in adult life must have been stifled ("but I want my unicorn back"). Elsewhere Dose reiterates the idea that standardized education is a model for broader conformity and again compares the student to a manufactured product, taking a condescending adult voice: "oh, ha ha ha, he's so creative/ but he's no XL57." And he takes a poke at the atmosphere of competition and obedience fostered by the oft-arbitrary grading system: "that's funny/ yours says 'good job,' too." This track, which follows "Revenge of the Fern," an allegorical diatribe about the destruction of the natural environment by science-driven technologies in which he asserts, "state of the art/ more like desire of the kings," establishes Dose as a person who does not care for authoritarian society and its crimes against life, regardless of what Drucker may or may not claim elsewhere.

Placed in the context of an album with those two songs, some of Dose's other lyrics seem even more anarchistic than they otherwise would. His phrase "man's endless pursuit of absolute stuff" ("Directions to My Special Place"), the almost anarcho-primitive query "must you be in a lab to feel a part of advancement?" ("Crayon Sharpener"), and his clear mocking, in the guise of a brilliantly altered Shakespeare quotation, of consumerism for "Joyful Toy of 1001 Faces" ("in a theme park, packed with debit-and-credit crysalises/ hark, what plush burgundy marketing ploy upon yonder libido breaks?") take on heightened significance when one strips any absurd claim of artistry conceived without regard for the social environment from which it springs.

More nuanced social commentary comes from the unlikely source of Cincinatti's Illogic, who has always leaned toward Christian allegory, battle rhymes, and fairly generalized words of wisdom; still, he defines *salary* in a rather caustic and anti-capitalist fashion as "the substance of stupidity, ripping the world apart" for "Screenplay." This may lead one to wonder whether Illogic has pondered the role of (a substantially stupid) belief in the Judeo-Christian god in extracting salaries and pushing humans to rip the living world apart.

Pre-millennial tension may have driven Mos Def, who may no longer be an indie-label phenom but warrants credit nonetheless, to compose the brilliant "New World Water" for his first solo album in 1999. Much as the spate of bleak late-Nineties films likely would never have seen wide release in any other period, Mos Def's anti-corporate gem slipped through in a year when chaos seemed impending. In 1997 or 2001 a similar blend of blistering social critique and grim prophecy may have been rejected by a record label just establishing (as Rawkus was then) mainstream viability. (Ras Kass, for example, probably was not responsible for Patchwerk's decision in 1998 to exclude "The Music of Business"-a white-label classic best summarized by the line "a record deal? that shit's a loan with a fucked-up interest rate"-from his second album.) Moreover, the presence of a sure-fire hit in "Ms. Fat Booty," from the same LP, may have convinced the label head(s) to let Mos slide. Or maybe I'm speculating wrecklessly. Regardless, "New World Water" came out, and, as of 2004, few have heeded its lyrics, which are essentially a musical echo of warnings issued for decades by human-rights and environmental organizations about the shortage of clean water on the planet. Mos rhymes that H2O "used to be free/now it costs you a fee/because oil tankers spill their loads when they cross over seas" and asserts that he'd rather have a water tank than a bank, a point of reason generally not grasped by the purportedly rational denizens of advanced-capitalist nations. A bank and its contents have virtually no intrinsic value but become objects of obsession in a bizarre and degenerate economic superstructure; meanwhile fresh water, one of the few things without which humans absolutely cannot survive (not even, in fact, for a week) is valued so poorly in most economies that their command centers (private firms, corporations, governmental agencies, et cetera) routinely render it unfit for human consumption. This process is described poetically by the emcee in question: "Americans waste it on some leisure shit/and other nations be desperately seeking it/the bacteria washing up on their beaches said/'don't drink the water' so they can't wash their feet with it...there are places where TB is as common as TV/'cause foreign-based companies go and get greedy/the type of cats who pollute a whole shoreline/then purify and sell it for $1.25." If the profit motive and its attendant machinations do not cause the extinction of all life forms on this planet larger and more complex than viruses, then this survival will come despite the best efforts of destructive greed and mechanical apathy as practiced by the likes of the United States Army and Exxon.

So in conclusion — OK, I'll give you a few more agit-rap quotations before I wrap this up. El-P poses as the United States of America for "Patriotism" and succinctly puts the lie to the claim that we live in a democracy: "I'm lovin' it/keep the people guessing who I'm running with/control the population and hide behind sacred covenants." Anyone familiar with the invocation of "executive privilege" or, more commonly, "national security" when secret misdeeds committed by the rulers come to light should appreciate this statement. SoCal soldier Lmno dropped an unappreciated single ("Courage" b/w "Hit the Fence") in the late Nineties, and "Hit the Fence" includes the subversive lines "the Government knows it can't control everyone's mind/...control is a money collector/affect her and his nourishment/which furthers them from being content/economic food chain/what's your role in the cycle?" Indeed, the withholding of necessities makes for a very persuasive tool in the unfree market. "Live from the Plantation," Mr. Lif's paean to wage slavery, includes an (unconscious?) parallel to the anarchist criticism of work ("life is a gift to be enjoyed every second, every minute/ is temporary, not infinite/ yet I find myself looking at the clock/ hoping for the day to fly by") that, if nothing else, poetically asserts an idea that should be common sense. Lif later makes the rhetorically impermissible but undeniably true statement that "the purpose of our life is just to serve the economy." Immortal Technique expresses a similar sentiment on "Harlem Streets": "check to check, constant struggle to make the payments/ your whole life, wondering where your day went/ the subway stays packed, like a multicultural slave ship/ it's rush hour 2:30 to 8, non-stopping/ people coming home after corporate sharecropping." In fact, even if nothing else were wrong with our socio-economic system, the laboring majority would still carry the burden of supporting a non-contributing class of virtual aristocrats through those tributes that we call profits. In order that a small minority may live in leisure and opulence, the rest of the yokels must sacrifice the time that otherwise would constitute their personal lives on the altar of Work. Finally, the Los Angeleno 2Mex strikes an anarcho-primitivist note on "Day and Night" when he asserts that "the only way to return to natural land/ is that all buildings, no matter how tall/ all fall to pillars of sand"; this sentiment is not dissimilar from the impulse that led an anarchist I once met to have emblazoned on one arm a tattoo of the collapse of a city's downtown buildings. If John Zerzan and his ilk are correct, humankind will not be free of unjust social constraints until not just governments and corporations but also machines and other artifices like skyscrapers are destroyed.

Chapter 19: The Aryan Hiphop Movement

I'd heard the rumors, whispered by artists and fans alike, regardless of their ethnicity or race. The tales were absurd on every level I could imagine; yet they held me fascinated, reeking as they did of that degenerate socio-cultural beast known as racism. I suppose that, given the both the expansion of hiphop culture and the stubborn persistence of racial bigotry in the United States, some kind of intersection was inevitable. And there have long been racial issues in hiphop, such as (among other phenomena) the extant (though fading) belief that rap should be exclusively made by African-Americans[44], those infamous anti-Semitic remarks Professor Griff made in 1989 or '90, the venomous diatribes about Koreans and "crackers" on Ice Cube's *Death Certificate*, and the inappropriate appropriation of the term *nigga* by hiphop fans who aren't black. Meanwhile, a great deal of the mainstream, white-dominated media's hysteria-mongering nonsense over "gangsta" rap in the Eighties and Nineties both fed and fed from European-Americans' paranoid conception of a young, black, male bogeyman. Still, when some individuals insisted that there was a small "scene" based on white-supremacist rap, the idea seemed even less plausible than some of

---

[44] For a succinct summary of this mentality, witness the chorus from the Figures of Speech song "Don't Get It Twisted" (off the mostly amazing 1995 Project Blowed compilation): "hiphop is not for crackers."

the more popular urban legends and Internet hoaxes I'd read about. Would "white power" proponents, who already have tiny niches in the punk and metal genres of rock, branch out to hiphop music? Then I remembered a letter printed in *The Source* in or around 1993, written by someone claiming to be a white guy from Boston, which alleged that the writer and his friends listened to thuggish rap tapes because they enjoyed hearing black males discuss killing each other. At the time I assumed it was phony, but now I wasn't so sure.

So I did some research on the Web and got nothing but the usual white-supremacist and white-separatist bullshit. Then I came across some message-board bullshit where ignoramuses claimed that several members of the Anticon collective were/are racist whiteys. And I read some hand-wringing comments about El-P's use of the n-word in an old song[45] as well as some complaints about certain African-American rappers' complaints about the number of white youths at their shows. But I found no evidence of anything resembling KKK-type rap. Further investigation was needed.

I attended some meetings of a neo-Nazi group. Nothing there. I went to a Klan rally. Again, nothing. But I finally found some proverbial gold in the pan at a racist-skinhead punk show. Some dude in the back was wearing an Insane Clown Posse t-shirt; I asked him if he listened to "white rap," he responded that most white rappers were "race traitors" who collaborated with non-white musicians and engineers, and then he handed me a pamphlet. Inside was a catalog of "white pride" CDs in

---

[45] El-P dropped the n-bomb on "Juvenile Technique" back around 1994.

various genres, including some described as rap. I was incredulous at the possibility of success, though tempered by the fact that the catalog had a P.O. box for an address.

I ordered all five pro-white rap albums and received them about two weeks later. The music sounded ridiculous and terrible: boring-ass beats, technically inept vocals, and lyrics that would be brilliantly absurdist if they weren't so serious. I sent "fan" letters, which led to e-mail contact, which led to phone calls and eventually a clandestine meeting with an Aryan named Shaemus. This guy looked like a model for an old Nazi propaganda poster: pinkish-white skin, golden-blond hair, blue eyes, chiseled features. He took his coffee with a good deal of cream, informing me that he refused to drink black coffee. Also, he wore a pair of white Nikes, a white t-shirt, and blue jeans. I didn't ask, but I assumed his underwear and socks were also white. He—OK, this has gone far enough. I apologize to my readers, all four of you. There is no Aryan-rap underground (as far as I know, anyway). I have never even searched for one. I had intended for this chapter to be fictional but obvious and humorous in the way that the "hiphop backpacker" story is, but that just isn't working for me. Oops. I think I have to reboot this section with a new paragraph and a new attitude, minus the snarky sarcasm.

So, in review, all of the stuff I wrote about the intersection of racism and rap is true, including that letter to *The Source* (the authenticity of the letter itself may never be established, of course), Professor Griff's anti-Semitism, etc.; but all of the Aryan Hiphop Nation material is fictional. I would like to discuss race and rap in earnest, though, and I can hardly imagine a better forum than the present one.

Now, I am going to attempt to stop being facetious long enough to admit that, as a white man, I occupy a still-precarious position in hiphop culture. While Whitey has long since been accepted as an inevitable part of this phenomenon called hiphop, rap is a musical form originally eked out by a denigrated group within a society that remains significantly racist despite decades of slow improvement. I am a member of the working class, jogging on the same hamster wheel as countless generations of my ancestors, and I have lived from paycheck to paycheck for my entire adult life, which has coincided with an era of vastly diminished earning power for average U.S. wage-and-salary servants; still, I benefit financially, usually in the job market, from a bias that has changed from open and oppressive to unspoken and slightly less oppressive. Not all working-class whites are aware at all times of their covert racial privileges, but working-class blacks never forget. Racism has long been a useful tool for the white capitalist power structure, one more means to dividing the hoi polloi, but when an African-American employee sees an equally qualified European-American co-worker get promoted first or make more money per hour he or she sees a beneficiary of racial discrimination first and a fellow capitalist pawn second.

Whites, on average, make more money than blacks with equivalent qualifications, face a "criminal justice" system that tilts in their favor, and so on. They/we already co-opted the blues and jazz, two monumental African-American creations, thereby adding to the list of grievances, and so black reluctance to admit whites to the Church or Temple of Hiphop is understandable. I think I cringed when I first heard Mikah 9 say "just like the white man, getting too greedy" on "Bullies of the Block" (from *Inner City Griots*), but I have to remind myself that, although not all white persons in this country stand at the absolute pinnacle of political-economic power, *only* white persons do. If one were to make lists of the five most powerful members of the federal government (President, Vice President, Speaker of the House, Senate Majority Leader, and Chief Justice) and the five wealthiest individuals in the U.S. on any given day in the nation's history, every person named would be white. The main trait I have in common with those guys is my skin color. LeRoi Jones may have been exaggerating when he called white rock musicians thieves of the blues tradition who make music devoid of authenticity,[46] but his contention that the blues and jazz were created exclusively by and for blacks remains valid for rap's parallel situation. Whether at the plantation or the fast-food window or the prison job, *et al*, the black laborer has received relatively little in return for his/her contributions to white-owned society, and thus emerges the desire to keep something valuable that blacks created as a black-only thing. I, like everyone from Paul Wall to Virtuoso, must never forget that I am an outsider with access to an important outlet constructed by and for blacks.

---

[46] In "The Changing Same (R & B and New Black Music)," 1966, included in his *Black Music*.

Chapter 20: A New Yorker Packs the House in Maine

The homey Ben and I arrive at Free Street Taverna in Portland around 9:15, and the place is dead. Louis Logic is slated to appear tonight, but maybe this town is unfamiliar with his music. Actually, I've never heard even one song from dude; so I'm here on the strength of word-of-mouth props. I get a beer, and we take a table near some of the relatively numerous cute chicks who would appear in the bar tonight.

Then nothing much happens for like two hours. I talk to some local acquaintances for a minute (that means you, Brzowski and DJ Mayonnaise), consume my entire microbrew, talk shit about movies with Ben, meet a friend of his, and snicker at a scene at the next table (a visibly inebriated guy is trying to pick up a young woman while her boyfriend has left the table to smoke a cigarette or something; she informs him that she and her female companion are lesbians). We grow restless despite the rap classics spinning on the turntables up front (this venue is so small that patrons have to walk in front of the stage when they enter), the opening act is a local group I've seen before, and I begin to utter some typical Scribe shit, like "Louis Logic had better not suck, cuz I'm getting tired of waiting to be entertained" or "if this show is wack, I'm holding you (whoever I happened to be speaking to) personally responsible"; I cannot recall my exact words. But the li'l place gets packed, and I slowly realize the performer has some fans.

When dude finally takes the stage at 11:45 or something, I'm nearly ready to dis him because I came too early for his show, which seems reasonable to me. He declares "Wow, color me surprised," in reference to a turnout larger than a New Yorker might expect at a small tavern in Maine. Then he launches into a series of humorous songs about sex, love, alcohol abuse, and pubic hair removal. Hardly the most political rapper around, though he does one race-themed song that he insists is not about President Bush, which is funny because it clearly includes some shots at him. Anyway, the emcee's stage presence is great, as he comes off like the friendly, flirtatious, funny guy at a party who never lacks for company. Louis's songs are somewhat novelty-ish, but that hardly bothers me (having never heard any of them) or the members of the crowd who have lyrics memorized and shout requests for their favorites. The cute blond chick (the one from the preceding paragraph) and her two cute friends dance to his music, some among the audience, including myself, laugh at his more pointed rhymes and between-song commentary, and a couple of dozen rap fans clamor toward the front of a tiny stage as if a pop star were in the house. But it's a man who has no Billboard hit in rotation on any Clear Channel station and no video getting played to death on any Viacom network. After the performance, fans push up on the stage to buy his record and maybe shake his hand, and he has to ask them politely to give him some space.

When Greg Tate declared in 1996[47] that there was no such

---

[47] On his slam poem or song "What Is Hiphop?" from the compilation *Flippin' the Script*, which also includes a short interlude by Mikah 9 called "Regurgitations."

thing as "alternative rap" because either it's hiphop or it isn't shit, he wasn't quite correct. Even then there was a skeleton of the hiphop scene that now provides an alternative to the corporate-controlled, risk-averse, talent-optional beast that passes for contemporary rap. By 1995 Los Angeles had the Project Blowed, New York had an array of independent labels (such as Fondle 'Em and Raw Shack), the Bay Area had DIY-touring and DIY-releasing acts (such as Blackalicious and the Mystik Journeymen), the Twin Cities had a vibrant scene virtually unknown outside of the Midwest, and Cincinatti had an embryonic version of Scribble Jam. In 2005 hiphop music has taken a quantum leap toward a decentralized state of being, and even the present pessimist has reason to hope that a decade hence the major labels, the corporate radio networks, and the mainstream music periodicals, *et al*, will have lost the ability to act as profit-leeching middlemen, taste arbiters and de facto censors for rap musicians and their fans.

Chapter 21: Sado-Rap

So an MC comes along in 1997 that pretty much no one outside of greater Detroit has heard of with a tape called *The Slim Shady EP* and lights up the underground. He takes part in infamous battles in Cincinnati and Los Angeles, shows up on radio shows and mix tapes with memorized-but-memorable "freestyles," and manages to almost shock listeners with a song about murdering his daughter's mother performed with touches of babytalk. Dr. Dre signs him, and several platinum albums follow.

If Eminem had not come up from the underground scene, I'd have no reason to discuss him herein. (In fact, in case anyone should doubt his pedigree, it should be noted that Eminem's self-released mini-album/demo was reviewed for such underground-oriented outlets as *Stress* and *Truehiphop.com* and that Marshall Mathers's '97 battle opponents included such indie-rap stalwarts as Otherwise, DoseOne, and Juice.) If Eminem sucked, I'd feel no need to discuss him at all. But he's one of the most compelling and talented rappers I've ever heard — and I listen to the gamut from emo-goth rap to nihilist hardcore rap — although that's still not reason enough to pontificate here. My purpose (if there must be one) is to expound on my dual feelings toward his music and what it represents. If I didn't speak English, I suppose I could listen to gems like "there's three things I hate: girls, women, and bitches" without qualm, as Eminem delivers almost every line with impeccable cadence and enunciation. However, our shared language forces certain moral choices. Should I condone the generally high musical quality or condemn Eminem's misanthropic tendencies?

At this point, Marshall Mathers's homophobic and misogynous lyrics have been well-documented (and properly, if not widely, criticized), but most of the calling out of Eminem has come from outside hiphop, with his detractors including techno musician Moby[48], anti-sexism activist Jackson Katz[49], music history professor Elizabeth Keathley[50], and *Village Voice* columnist Richard Goldstein[51] (Tori Amos, who covered "'97 Bonnie and Clyde" for her album *Twelve Little Girls*, seems ambivalent about Eminem himself despite her clear disdain for the norms of sexist violence that he encourages in his music[52]); within rap's hypermasculine ethos, a man helping women and gays defend themselves from verbal abuse is subject to taunts of "captain save-a-hoe" and "faggot" (which was the essence of Eminem's response to Moby[53]). As a somewhat pro-feminist male who also has had many queer friends and co-workers, I'm disgusted with the amount of gay-bashing and woman-hating bile percolating in hiphop. It's much simpler when MC Ignorant Self-Hating Quasi-Fascist treats women like seminal receptacles or threatens to kill gay men, since I'm unlikely to ever listen to his crappy records. When Slim Shady ends the brilliantly conceived "Guilty Conscience" with the celebrated murder of a male character's cheating wife, however, I'm conflicted. While it is indeed only a song (and a very creative one) and neither Dr. Dre nor Eminem has ever been accused of murder, it seems

---

[48] Their circa-2002 feud was quite public, but in case you missed it, do a Google search.
[49] Katz includes a scathing critique of Eminem among his essays collected in *The Macho Paradox* (2006).
[50] Keathley provides "A Context for Eminem's 'Murder Ballads'" in volume four, issue two (the fall 2002 issue) of the musicology journal *Echo*.
[51] The June 12 and November 13, 2002, issues of the *Voice* feature his analysis of Slim Shady's popularity.
[52] For example, the Atlantic Records press release, archived in a few places on the Internet, for that album in 2001 included Amos's comment that "people are getting into the music and grooving along to a song about a man who is butchering his wife."
[53] This would be on the hit single "Without Me" (2002).

to encourage violence against women—and that comes within a context of widespread *actual* brutality perpretrated by men against women in the United States (and elsewhere, of course). Furthermore, sentiments like "[I] went to gym in the eighth grade/ [and] raped the women's swim team" (from "Just Don't Give a Fuck") and Eminem's exhortation to "rape sluts" ("Who Knew") are not humorous exaggerations or cathartic expressions of anger. They're hateful and wrong. Thus I'm left repeating the waffling decision I once made about Ice (racist and misogynist) Cube: enjoy the creative and engaging songs ("Stan" or "The Product") and dis the abhorrent bullshit ("Kim" or "Black Korea"). And if anyone tries to call me out on this compromise, they'd better be prepared with a damn good argument, although I reserve the right to change my mind eventually and abstain from their music altogether.

Lest anyone be misled into assuming that underground rap today has no overt misogynists, I must note that the popular Brooklyn rapper-producer and general DIY entrepreneur Necro, who has released several of his own albums and DVDs on his own small label and gained a considerable following, largely on the strength of his live performances, devotes his lyrics almost entirely to descriptions of interpersonal violence, often directed at women. One can pick almost any track from Necro's catalog and hear graphic representations of the brutalization of women, from the glorification of sexual control in "The 12 King Pimp Commandments" to the imagination of serial rape, dismemberment, and murder in "Do the Charles Manson." I do not exaggerate when I say that nearly every song in his ouevre is like this—it is almost as if Necro decided to dedicate a musical career to the advocacy of violence, especially against women. Making matters worse, he draws out despicable rhyme-form fantasies from collabators, such as Ill Bill, who normally opt for other lyrical subjects and thereby drags other denizens of the mostly intelligent independent hiphop scene into the cesspool of misogyny with him.[54] To be certain, other rappers outside the mainstream have offered a few works with female-bashing content; but Saafir ("Worship the D," off *Boxcar Sessions*), Del the Funky Homosapien ("Boo Boo Heads," *No Need For Alarm*) , Ras Kass ("Drama," *Soul On Ice*), and Volume 10 ("Tricks-n-Hoes," *Hiphopera*) included just one song apiece on albums otherwise lacking sexist commentary and, furthermore, only one of those tracks (Del's contribution) is an exhortation to brutality.

Those rap fans who might defend Eminem/D-12 and Necro/Circle of Tyrants on the grounds that I am taking their lyrical content too literally or too seriously ought to bear in mind that millions of girls and women in this country are the living survivors of rape or battery by men and that many others are murdered by men every year. Or they could try an easy little exercise. Listen to an Eminem song wherein he describes violence against women and substitute "Jew" or "kike" for every word that refers to a woman, e.g., "I put kikes at risk with a knife like this." The result is chillingly Nazi-esque. Similarly, they could try replacing white Necro's misogynous references to women with racist terms for black persons; his lyrics would thus change from talk of murdering

---

[54] Have I mentioned that Necro bit his style from another rapper? Anyone who is familiar with Kool G Rap's signature rhyming pattern and cadence can hear an obvious emulation on every Necro album.

"bitches" to fantasies of killing "darkies," and his fanbase would shrink to include only pro-lynching KKK members. The cultural consequence would be different, although the object is dehumanized in an identical manner. The repetition of venomous words may indeed have a quietly destructive power when delivered to listeners of a certain bent, and I will not silently abide by the propagation of hateful music.

Chapter 22: The Bus Ride

So I guess I'll use their real names here. Fuck it. May as well just toss the veil of pseudonyms to the floor. Many in the underground know these individuals by the names on their birth certificates, not their record covers, and those who do not should find this story a poignant slice of life or a picaresque allegory and appreciate it as such. This little tale doesn't need fictional embellishment, although I may change a few details, if for no other reason than that my aptitude for recall is imperfect. Furthermore, the two friends described herein are unlikely to object to my use of their middle names—neither goes by his first name—for my lifted-from-real-life characters. And one of them loves to read his own press, so to speak, so he'll probably be amused with the idea of seeing his name in a story that may stay in print long after we're dead. And the female in this yarn—well, as of 2003 I haven't seen her in five years and don't even remember her surname. So allow me to relate some touching anecdotes from that oddly innocent period of my life when I wasn't completely bitter about my life or simmering with a sustained rage at our social system.

Shit, I've explained my presence in this unique urban area enough times to enough persons for enough reasons that I feel like a kid who shows up at school with his leg in a cast after a vacation spent skiing. How and why I came to San Francisco all the way from Maine. The critical part to understand is that I'd longed to get away from Greater Portland for a number of years, starting when I was fifteen, if I remember correctly, when I wanted to go to a college or university in Boston and then move to New York after graduation. Boston changed to Atlanta, Saint Louis, or Richmond-Norfolk with time, but it didn't matter. After getting rejected by both Emory College and Washington University and finding my finances insufficient for Norfolk State University, I ended up staying home, in essence, and going to the University of Southern Maine, just down Route 25 from the house I'd lived in since the second grade.

Right after my freshman year I met Tim (his middle name, remember), a fellow artisan in my field (which should go without saying at this point). After an initial period of mutual suspicion and preening egoism (let's just say that, while I hadn't honed my craft as well as he had, I still felt that my work was more important), we became friends. This was 1997, and we were both nineteen. (We would later learn that we had been born only nineteen days apart in the same town (Portland, of course).) In early 1998 I met his purported best friend Brandon, who was staying in Beantown with his lover. We didn't exactly "hit it off" right away, but, again, we became friends (I would later learn that he had been born about six weeks after me, in Virginia) with time. (At this point we were all twenty, by the way.)

In the second semester of my sophomore year I started to plan a summer in New York City, that metropolis I'd admired for as long as I could remember. (New York seemed to be the setting for an inordinate proportion of the books, movies, comics, and rap songs I'd been exposed to by then.) I hoped to take summer classes at NYU and stay at a youth hostel in Manhattan. My parents hated the idea, naturally. Then Tim mentioned that his long-delayed move to San Francisco now had a target date of mid-May. And Brandon was supposed to roll with him out there, at least temporarily. Now that was an idea. I told my parents about it. They seemed to hate it even more than the New York thing.

"I'll be back in late August for the fall semester, Ma," I explained.

"You'll never come back, Zachary," my mother responded. (My dad thought I was going to cross over, if you know what I mean, in San

Francisco.)

"Besides, I'm not sure about it yet," I added.

As the semester approached its end, Tim's plan became closer to a reality. He was going to take a bus out West and stay with some dude he kinda knew. I asked if he minded a fellow traveler.

"Nah, man, it'll be cool. We can kick it in Frisco," he said.

By the middle of May we had definite departure date of June 6th, and when D-Day came the three of us climbed onto a Greyhound bus in Forest City with a few bags of necessities (and my suitcase, which they dissed), ready for a three-day journey across the continent. We passed into New Hampshire—a state I despised to an irrational extent—and I was already bored when we arrived in Portsmouth. It was going to be a really long ride, I realized then. The seats were comfortable, at least, and actually much less cramped than the fucking coach-class seats on airliners. And Tim had brought some sandwiches, which was nice, but they became squashed and unacceptable to all save Brandon, who had even less money than us. I think he might have eaten those sandwiches even if he had had more money, though. Didn't really give a fuck, that guy.

We changed vehicles in Boston, sitting in a line with our bags (and my suitcase) for an hour or two while we waited for the next bus driver to get ready or whatever. This was where Vicki got on the bus, but it's not where she enters my story. Later for her. Brandon told me about Saul Williams, whose poem-songs I hadn't heard or read yet. We cracked some jokes about a rapper and his crew, native to the Beantown area, who all used an abundance of big words in their lyrics but didn't really say anything of substance.

"Is that Arcane?" (except I used his actual nom de plume) I asked Tim, who had met the rapper himself, when a vaguely Irish-looking hiphop kid walked by in the station. The three of us exchanged some mock verses.

"My strontium-90 style surpasses the supernumerary/I transform cold-fusion microphones with my vocabulary": these or some similar sentiments were expressed. The local-rapper wisecracks became a theme to be revisited at several other cities.

The bus traveled through Connecticut (the only time I've ever been there). I don't recall whether it stopped there or not, but we stayed on the mutherfucker either way. Then we reached NYC, the gothic metropolis that in recent years had seen its main borough gentrified and stripped of charisma. We changed busses in Manhattan, mocking the style of a different artist here (but not, it should be noted, the same individual that Tim would later have a feud with) as we waited. I'd never been to New York, of course, but these fucks had been there several times already, including one weekend during the previous April. We rode through sections of Manhattan and the Bronx and maybe Queens or Brooklyn, and I felt a little disappointed with the Big Apple.

We hit Newark, and by then it was dark. Newark loomed ugly from my perspective, but perhaps the station was just in a bad neighborhood. We didn't get out. I ate some of whatever crap I had brought (probably pretzels) and drank some "quarter waters" from the case I had. Couldn't sleep. Couldn't concentrate enough to read. I listened to Nas or Professor Griff (don't ask me about that choice, please) or Volume 10 or Fiona Apple (my professed soulmate at the time) on my Walkman in the dark of the bus, across the aisle from the two seats where my companions reclined.

Things were pretty quiet on the bus in general and among this particular trio as we rolled into Pennsylvania (the only occasion in my life so far when I would visit this state, along with most of the states we'd pass through), and we parked at a rest stop somewhere near Allentown. Brandon wanted to stay in his seat (probably to sleep, since he had done this trip a few times before and had learned how to sleep on long rides), but Tim and I strolled into a diner. I don't know what I ordered, as I was not yet vegan but in the process of slowly eliminating dairy products from my diet. Tim was stubbornly lacto-ovo, and I think he ordered toast and scrambled eggs. He interrogated the waiter (she was a woman, but I refuse to reify the term waitress, which implies that females who do the same job as male waiters somehow need a different, feminized job title, as with actress and poetess, *et al*) about the food-preparation facilities, wanting reassurance that his food wasn't cooked on the same griddle as animal flesh. She told him meat was cooked separately from things like eggs and pancakes, although I assumed that this was just to shut him up. He seemed satisfied with this response, either way. When the waiter returned with our beverages, Tim had removed the elastic band that held his shoulder-length hair back. He had a mischievous look in his eyes that only those who know him can recognize. He asked the server if the diner had an extra elastic band somewhere that he could have for his hair. She said "no, we don't," and he dropped the subject. As she walked away I asked him why he wanted to harass this woman, who was just trying to do her job. He responded with a bizarre explanation about how he wanted to test her customer-service skills as they related to customers she would never see again. This experiment, illogical and pointless to me, made sense to Tim, I guess. The public at large was a source of great amusement and education for him.

After sunrise in Ohio, which came around the time we left Cleveland, which had the oddest assemblage of humanity I'd ever seen at its Greyhound station and wherein I made some stupid comment about the possibility of seeing members of Bone Thugs N Harmony walking by the window, the unrested pair I traveled with began getting anxious and a tad obnoxious. They started playing a beat tape on Brandon's portable stereo and freestyling fake gangsta raps. I found it funny at first, although the sheer repetition over the next two days would kill the humor value for me (not so for them). Brandon started loudly reciting "it ain't me, mutherfucker, it ain't me", from Atmosphere's classic "Scapegoat," at random intervals. Ohio was really ugly, with all the images of post-industrial decay—in towns like Dayton—that I'd previously seen only in magazines now in my face. Abandoned factories, et cetera.

After Ohio my memory of the trail becomes fuzzy. A look at a map of the USA would lead me to believe we passed through Indiana at some point, yet I remember nothing about seeing that state. I do recall Illinois, specifically Chicago, wherein I relived the disappointment I'd felt at seeing New York. Tim said we were probably just in a boring part of the Windy City, but wherever we were was somewhat desolate. There was virtually no traffic of any kind, and the only humans we saw outside the bus station were some homeless men hustling newspapers. I bought a copy of Chicago's main daily paper from one guy and tipped him a dollar, prompting an eyeroll from Tim. We had to walk several blocks to find a place that had restrooms (the bus station's restrooms looked pretty nasty), which turned out to be Harold's Chicken Shack, with a large picture on its window depicting a guy with an axe chasing a chicken. Tasteless, really. We walked some more and found a sandwich shop or deli to eat at.

Somewhere in the Midwest I spotted a cute young female on the bus, thinking to myself that she'd been on the bus with us for a while; since New York, maybe. Tim hadn't seen her, and he had made some remark about some vaguely raver-looking chick (who, along with her boyfriend, we later discovered, was going all the way to San Francisco as well, and they had started in Boston) being the only "remotely fuckable" female on the bus. Brandon harangued me about some of my concurrent musical tastes, convincing me that Gangstarr and Professor Griff were wack. He also gave me a dub of a 90-minute L.A. underground rap tape. I'm not sure how, but the topic of who I'd rather fuck, Tim or Brandon, given some circumstance where I absolutely had to choose, came up; after some harassment I chose Brandon.

Tim was reading a *Philosophy for Dummies*-type book. I think I was chipping away at *The Bonfire of the Vanities*. We ate from a large package of sunflower seeds I'd brought, knowing my comrades' fondness for them. They teased me about my quarter waters. ("Scribe always has to have some fruit punch," Tim said.) I suppose I was asking for it.

I'd never seen anything like the landscape of Iowa, ever. It was just flat for as far as I could see. We often passed through routes where there were miles of cornfields and virtually no buildings. No hills or mountains or lakes or towns or seashore. We'd spend hours on the road and the scenery wouldn't have any substantial change. For someone born and raised along a rugged coast, it felt like a kind of purgatory.

Somewhere in Iowa, at a rest stop, possibly in Iowa City, one of us talked to the cute female I'd noticed. Her name was Vicki; she came from Massachusetts, attended Boston University, was 18 or 19, and had been riding along with us since Boston. As all the passengers stepped back onto the vehicle I asked her if she wanted to sit in the empty seat beside me. She grabbed her bags and came back with us. She had wavy, brown hair and freckles on her nose. She'd been raised in a small town, and her blue-collar parents taught her to work hard and rewarded her by paying the exorbitant costs of B.U. We discussed our studies at our respective universities (me: philosophy and economics; her: art history and religion) and how we had been raised. She was gonna stay with a friend in San Francisco for three weeks and then return to some job in Mass. I quickly developed an infatuation with her that was most likely requited.

She thought she recognized Brandon from somewhere, and they figured out that she used to see him when he worked at a convenience store on BU's campus—his girl was a student there, too. An odd coincidence, I guess. Anyway, this being me here, the potential romance would have to get squashed one way or another. And this time it was my friends' boredom that did me in. They also seemed—I don't know if "jealous" is the right description, but probably annoyed that I had met a cute girl to hang out with on this boring-ass, three-day bus ride. They had left behind putative girlfriends back East. (Note: Tim's "shorty" had been in obvious denial when D-Day approached, apparently thinking that Tim would never go through with the drastic measure of moving across the country and leaving almost everything and everyone he knew behind; or else she thought it was one of Tim's jokes, taken to an extreme at her expense.)

Soon after Vicki and I started conversing (maybe it was around the time that we learned that we were both vegetarians), Tim and Brandon started harassing me from across the aisle. Yep, regardless of what could have happened between Vicki and me and of whether it was their intenton or not, they were doing it. Cock-blocking. When they heard me make some thinly-veiled compliment about Vicki's looks, they laughed, audibly. They took turns whispering remarks to me (I was sitting on the outside, while she had the window seat) across the aisle; things like "ask her if she enjoys casual sex", "grab her tits"; and, as she napped, "molest her". Vicki couldn't hear them, but she could see my agitation, which reflected poorly on my temperament. I felt acute embarrassment at their behavior and did my best to ignore them.

When they weren't giving me shit, they were doing more of their thug-mocking raps and cursing loudly, to the palpable irritation of nearby passengers. A woman, sitting directly in front of this duo with her young son, turned around to request that they cease their "obscenities". They giggled and ignored her. At the next rest stop someone complained to the bus driver, who informed Tim and Brandon that they would be ejected if they continued such behavior. Jesus Christ, I thought, they're gonna get kicked off the bus, and I'm gonna be alone in San Francisco. Still, it would have prevented them from fucking with my, as Tim put it, "kicking game" to Vicki, thus I had mixed feelings on the matter.

Anyway, they ceased being such an aggravation to strangers but wouldn't quit fucking with me until we reached California. A little distance from some stop in the boondocks of flyover country, the four of us tried to smoke some green that Vicki had brought; we couldn't get it lit, though, thanks to some strong gusts. It was considerably warmer in the so-called Heartland than it had been back in New England and also quite humid. After a couple of days on the road I needed a shave, and we all felt the need to bathe, although no facilities for such things were available to us. Tim and Brandon joked that they would get SCRUB LIFE tattoos.

Somewhere out in the box states Tim encouraged me to ask Vicki to hang out in San Francisco. I told him I might, but I explained that I felt like a jackass because my friends were teasing me so much in front of her.

"Don't exaggerate, dude," he replied.

At Bubblefuck, Wyoming, outside a Western-looking "general store," Tim and I posed for photos in front of a parked sheriff's department cruiser, throwing up the "W" in highly ironic fashion. Brandon had the camera, and he also took a shot of Vicki's lovely face. Wyoming was as strange as the cornfield country to me, with mountains and huge fucking rocks and desert-like terrain all over the place. But it was much more visually appealing than Nebraska.

We hit Utah, also hella flat, and I was gripped with the irrational conviction that something terrible would happen to me here and I'd never get to California. I was sure my radical ass would somehow offend someone somewhere in this bastion of conservativism and Mormonism. This anxiety, I suppose, must have been influenced by my sleep deprivation—after two full days of riding I hadn't been able to sleep. I don't remember if any of my companions had slept yet, but it was dark when we stopped in Salt Lake City. We were gonna be there for a few hours and decided to wander the city. We split with "my girl," as Brandon and Tim referred to her, and walked along astoundingly-clean sidewalks that ran parallel to the widest streets I've ever seen. Brigham Young had dictated a specific width for the streets in Mormon country, we learned. Vicki, through methods inscrutable to us, found the three of us as we posed for sacrilegious pictures in front of some statues. The streets were eerily quiet. The people of this burg weren't exactly out living it up on this evening, true to form, and a convenience-store clerk explained to us that the whole state had really strict alcohol regulations for those who did choose to party. I was confounded by all this Mormon shiznit as well as Vicki's homing-pigeon act and thus very anxious to get the fuck out of Utah. All of us finally slept that night.

I think we woke up in Nevada. Regardless, Nevada came after Utah. The other three went into a McDonald's outlet, but I stayed on the bus. I had no interest in eating that crapola, even the meat-free items. Wheat-germ-and-spinal-cord patties or genetically-engineered poultry and hormone-injected dairy products? I'd rather fast. We went through Reno, which looked pretty unappetizing to me. I have since discovered that Reno is a very popular weekend hangout for Bay Area denizens, but I haven't returned for any reason. I tried to purchase a copy of Reno's morning paper, but the newsrack swallowed my change without letting me grab a paper. It must have been the third day of our sojourn, which was June 9th, and our destination was creeping up on us. I started to feel a slight urgency to get some sort of contact info from Vicki.

We stopped in Sacramento, which I remember being warm—or I could just be projecting my current knowledge of that area's climate onto my memory. We went to a burger spot that claimed to have been featured in a Quentin Tarantino film. I got some sort of vegetarian sandwich. Then we moved on to Vallejo, where we saw some dude who looked a bit like E-40, prompting me to make some sort of stupid wisecrack. The end of the journey was approaching. I was hungry, dirty, and tired, plus wary and uneasy about my big leap. We stopped again in downtown Oakland, which looked mostly as I had expected it to.

Then we crossed the Bay Bridge, quite the sight for a small-town kid, even though I'd visited Boston several times and Washington once. The view of San Francisco's Financial District highrises and Alcatraz as we entered the city was, for whatever reason, much more impressive to me than what I'd recently seen in New York and Chicago. We pulled into the bus station and shuffled out to grab our bags from beneath the coach. One of Brandon's bags was lost. He had to fill out a claim. The decisive moment came, and I let Vicki go with no more than a handshake or a hug (I forget which). Tim gave me the phone number for the apartment he and Brandon would be staying at. I walked out to the front of the Transbay Terminal and hailed a cab, a list of hostel addresses in hand.

Chapter 23: Coda

For the sixth consecutive year my dream of attending Scribble Jam again, soaking in Ohioan heat and magnificent rap, has been crushed by circumstances that I am certain will seem ridiculous when I lay on my deathbed and consider my life and chew on bitter, useless regrets. My fall-back plan of a brief vacation in New York City provoked a harshly negative response from my girlfriend, and we came to a sort of compromise wherein I get a two-day camping trip at a lake an hour from home. I haven't been camping in fifteen years, and I savor the idea of both a respite from my daily routine and a reunion with the outdoors. I recently had this absurd opinion that New York would be a fitting place to write the last chapter in a book about rap, given hiphop's origins there. But Scribe is nothing if not belligerently different, and thus a rustic retreat for composition about a distinctly urban phenomenon almost makes sense when he does it. Plus Saul Williams famously declared, on "Twice the First Time," that one must "extract the urban element that created it and let it open wide, countryside illustrated" and that "you ain't ever walked through the trees listening to 'Nobody Beats the Biz' and you ain't ever heard hiphop."

The sky is a summery blue, interrupted only by fluffy white clouds. Crickets sing. Crescent Lake ripples beneath countless evergreen trees, and nothing is plastered with advertising. I cook my tofu pups on charcoal, and I sleep in a tent. I am far from my shit job and very far from the Big Apple when I put Saul's dictum to the test with a battery-powered CD player and (why not?) his second album, itself an unusual combination of rock and rap. I think Williams might appreciate this venture, and he might even agree with my assessment here; a few tracks into the CD I feel I've introduced a noisy intrusion to the woods. No one else in the campground (in earshot, at least) is playing music, and both the mostly angry tone and the synthesizer-driven production of this album only exacerbate the out-of-place feeling. I'd forgotten about "Grippo" and its racial commentary, but its lyrics make it a fresh companion to the older piece mentioned above. The last chapter I revamped was the piece about racial issues in rap, and this song contains some sentiments that would frame my work nicely ("I gave hiphop to white boys when nobody was looking...replace the anger and repression with guilt and depression and it's yours") as well as an astro-poetic line that complements my little excursion to the forest ("I wanna show you what the stars are made of") because last night I was able to observe the stars for the first time in many years. I remember reading somewhere that supposedly melanin may come from some far-off solar system—I believe that would be Saul's inspiration for this lyric—and if that's true then it's fucked up because African-Americans disproportionately populate the urban areas where ambient light blots out the stars. I listen to some other artists, but despite that one song's brief intersection with my life, listening to music has done nothing to enhance my camping experience. I turn off the stereo.

A cute chipmunk (is there any other kind?) cautiously approaches my campsite. He chatters to himself, but after a minute or two I swear his small-mammal cackles have a specific rhythm. Furthermore, this rhythm reminds me of a famous hiphop beat.

"Microphone Fiend."

And did he just chirp something that sounded like "E-F-F-E-C-T"? I must look bewildered, since the chipmunk looks up from foraging in the nearby brush and snickers. I look around for other campers, but all of the sites near mine are vacant. The woodland creature walks toward me, coming to a halt at a close but safe distance.

"I'm rated R, this is a warning," he raps.

I'm dumbfounded. Flabbergasted. Speechless. The chipmunk does his high-pitched laughter thing again.

"I heard your portable stereo," he tells me. "I didn't recognize the artists, though. I'm into Rakim, The Roots, Outkast, Common when he still had Sense, Jurassic 5, *et cetera.*"

I ignore the obvious impossibilities of my present situation and respond.

"You had me until you mentioned J5. Anyway, I had no idea that--"

"I know, I know. But all mammals can speak. Unless we can't, and you're only imagining me."

A chipmunk who can talk, enjoys rap, and has a funny sense of metaphysics. That would be a typical product of my right cranial hemisphere in a reverie.

"Humanity is choking on its industrial fumes," he says. "Frogs are born with frightening deformities. Polar ice caps are melting. Your overlords wield enough weaponry to wipe all complex organisms, including themselves, off the face of the planet. I'd be surprised if anything more advanced than a virus survived a nuclear war. Sometimes it feels as though we are living in the last days, but when you people talk about the end of the world you only mean the extinction of humankind or, at most, all life on Earth. The big rock will keep on spinning and revolving around that commonplace star. And a bunch of young North Americans scat-barking into microphones make not a whisper audible from Alpha Centauri."

Then he scampers off and runs up a tree trunk.

Disoriented, I feel the need to do something to get my bearings. I step into my tent and change into my swim trunks for a quick dip in the lake. That might prove refreshing, I surmise. I stroll down to the beach area, remembering Sage Francis's smart reply to my "interview" question about whether growing up in New England made a significant difference in his development as an artist.

"I make more nature references than NYC rappers, and unintentionally so. There's a metaphor somewhere in that answer."

I ease myself into the water and wade in until it reaches chest height. The lake is just too damn cold for my blood, and I stand with my arms crossed and look down at my reflection. Then something inexplicable happens. My reflection stops being a reflection. My face looks a few years younger and seems to scowl at me. I shake my head vigorously, as though I can get the image out of my head, and dive into the cool water. I do not need much time to feel "refreshed" and soon remove my cold-blooded body from the lake.

I dry off and change back into shorts and a tee plus the obligatory baseball cap, and my bladder reminds me of its existence. I strut my way up to the bathroom and relieve myself, but before I can leave the place someone says "hey." I look around for another guy and conclude I must be the addressee.

"Someone talking to me?" I ask, trying not to sound like Robert De Niro.

A stall door swings open , and I stare myself in the face again. This self also looks a bit younger, maybe three years, but he isn't scowling.

"Get that stupid look off your face. You're too smart to look that dumb," he tells me.

"Being the inventor of neo-existentialism and post-postmodernism as well as the first individual to consciously fuse hiphop with existentialism and presumably rap's first anarchist philosopher, I feel I hold a unique position in the culture. Just pause for a moment and soak up some of the glorious rays of magnificence that I exude...feel great, don't they? Don't you feel blessed to share the planet with a man as ingenius as I am? It's amazing but true that, despite all of my greatness, I am still humble and beneficent enough to share my wisdom with the hoi polloi. In addition to my status as one of the absolute smartest humans in recorded history, I also hold the distinction of being the *most hiphop* genius ever.

"I am so hiphop that I got my pseudonym tatted on my chest. I am so hiphop that for a period of several months in 1999 I practiced freestyling every day for twenty minutes. I followed this with a period of roughly two years when I wrote lyrics or prose (mostly lyrics, of course) *every day*, missing maybe five days total during the span. I'm so rap-centric that in the spring of '94 I spent the last dollar I had before getting my first 'real' job on a cassette entitled *Illmatic*, which I then played so much that the tape became warped and eventually had to be tossed in the garbage (and replaced by the tenth-anniversary, remastered CD). I'm so hiphop that, even though I never listened to Rakim on a mountaintop, a few times in high school I played gangster rap on my Walkman while walking the path in the woods between my neighborhood and a local basketball court. I'm so hiphop that I've listened to Saafir on an airplane over the Rocky Mountains, Ras Kass on a bus through Nebraska, Black Moon in my car in Maine, and the Sebutones at work in San Francisco. I'm so hiphop that I read *The Source* in the glorious early 1990s and then had a subscription to *Rap Pages* (before that mag fell off, of course). I've seen parts of Snoop Dogg's *Girls Gone Wild* DVD, all of Master P's *I'm 'Bout It*, and every video from *The Chronic* and *Doggystyle*. I even sat through *Trespass, Posse, Set It Off*, and several other worthless, hiphop-targeted works of Hollywood marketing. I'm so hiphop that I grew up listening to rap despite living in Maine and having white skin—and that was long before rap hijacked the *Billboard* charts. I used to wear some Tommy Hilfiger clothing, mainly because Raekwon and Grand Puba said it was fresh. I could go on, but I think you get the point. Anyone who knows me well enough to have heard me wax negative about virtually everything could tell you that there are few things I like or love, and rap is one of those positive passions. And I'm a smart bastard, in case you hadn't heard. In conclusion, I am a genius who is obsessed with hiphop music, which says a lot in favor of rap's artistic merit."

Then my conceited doppelganger walks past me, out the door, and into oblivion.

I return to my campsite and crack open a can of soda to wash down some redskin peanuts. I gaze at the gorgeous clouds drifting to wherever and suddenly see myself from the inside of my computer monitor at home, typing a sentence about how I am staring at those clouds and seeing myself from the inside of my PC monitor.

I pass a few hours by relaxing the way I planned to, and at dusk I start a little fire to keep me warm through the cooler-than-usual August evening. I have the Red Sox game on the radio, not too loud for the other campers, but nevertheless one of them stops and asks me the score. The Sox are losing, of course, because their late-summer decline is practically a law of thermodynamics, and the guy resumes his stroll.

A few moments later someone else halts his walk on the dirt path when he reaches my camp, but this dude wants to hang out and listen to the game for a little while. I look him over quickly, deem him harmless, and oblige his request. He looks about thirty, unshaven and still dressed in shorts despite the post-sunset chill, with a baseball hat pulled low on his dome.

"I haven't seen a baseball game in years. By the way, my name's Chris," he tells me.

"I don't have cable TV, but I watch games here and there and listen on the radio a lot," I reply. "More into basketball and football, anyway. Oh, I'm Zachary."

"Did I hear some rap coming from this area this afternoon?" he asks.

"Yeah, I tried to keep the volume down, but—"

"It's all right, just a little surprising. I go camping for a week every summer and almost never hear any music, let alone hiphop. Who was that?"

"Saul Williams, mostly. A couple songs from Azeem and The Pharcyde, too."

"Yeah, I recognized 'Drop,'" he says and then leans in to whisper, "which goes really well with some pot. Got any, by chance?"

"No," I answer truthfully, "but I wish—"

I'm looking over at him as I speak and stop mid-sentence when I get my first good look at his face. His eye sockets appear to be empty, although it could be a trick of the light.

"Notice my lack of eyes? It's OK, I get all types of reactions. Probably I should get some glass ones, but I do not feel like doing something useless for myself just to accomodate the visually-capable. Fuck 'em. If I'm with my girl or out in public I wear a pair of very dark sunglasses, but that's it. I shot myself when I was 22 and ended up with minor skull damage and no eyeballs. It was a botched suicide attempt, not an accident. The one benefit is that I have really learned how to listen. Other than that, well, I lead a normal life, even though this doesn't make the day-to-day shit any easier."

I tell him he is starting to make me feel badly about my poor ear care, inflicting damage on my hearing with loud music and whatnot.

"Let me tell you something, bro. Don't feel guilt on my behalf. They're your ear drums. Just don't let me hear you saying 'rap sucks now' or 'rap is dead' or anything analogous. Yes, hiphop has an abundance of poseurs and carpetbaggers these days. When did it not? 1978? Anyone who claims that this takeover of hiphop music by jackasses is a recent development and that he/she no longer likes rap as a result has revealed him/herself as a new jack/jill. In 1991 Hammer and Vanilla Ice were toting platinum plaques, whereas the likes of Organized Konfusion, Third Bass, A Tribe Called Quest, Freestyle Fellowship and Del the Funky Homosapien dropped classic records but were lucky not to get dropped from their record labels. There probably were kids back then lamenting the death of hiphop, too. I've been hearing this bullshit myself since 1993, and I'm quite sick of it. Until such time as absolutely no talented rap artists remain I don't wanna hear this 'rap used to be great but sucks now' talk, because I can't hear all of the great music out there for all of the ignorant whining about the lack of great music out there."

I tell him I couldn't agree more.

"Hiphop is not dead, so shut up about it, right?" I offer.

"Yes, absolutely. Music is my greatest love. I live in Boston and go to my share of shows, usually with my girlfriend. Funny story, though, one night at the Middle East I was high as fuck off hashish and pure oxygen at a Perceptionists show when I ran into some cat who was claiming Portland. He said his name was Nomar Slevik, which I remember mainly because I'm a Sox fan and consequently asked if his stage name was inspired by Nomar Garciaparra. I don't remember his answer, though. Actually, I'm not sure if I even met him at that show or another one. I've seen Virtuoso a couple times there. Anyway, apparently we both admired Lindsay Lohan back then—I liked her voice, while he said she looked hot— and liked JD Walker's music. I said Jay did Everlast's style better than Everlast, but your boy pretended not to find my comment amusing enough to actually laugh."

I inform Chris that I also know this Nomar Slevik character, who once disagreed with me about whether kittens are counterrevolutionary (I continue to contend that adorable baby cats are simply not conducive to mass rebellion).

"Well, same night, I think, not that it matters, was when I met my good friend Vince, who happens to be at this campground with me and my girl and his girl. A tent for each couple, of course. Last night he told us about this time he did 'shrooms in Nevada. He had just blown some money at the blackjack table and the sports book, but it was only like $50 because he went in expecting to lose.

"So Vince and Jessica were staying in Reno and somehow managed to obtain psilocybin. Bored with gambling, which was not even the primary reason they had chosen Nevada, they drove out to some nearby rocky area and choked down some mushrooms. This was, I don't know, Vin's fifth time eating shrooms, but it was his girl's first experience; so she really opened up her frontal lobe for a couple of hours.

"She stared at one of the rocks for a while and described what she saw to Vince, who, for whatever reason, was barely even tripping, which enabled him to remember a lot of this stuff. Jess saw, in some sense of the word, images in the crevices of the rock and the shadows on it. One vision consisted of the faces of some political and economic leaders, like senators and CEOs and generals, with translucent skin that partly revealed reptilian scales and features. Another one was an alien, you know the kind that almost everyone who thinks they've seen an extraterrestrial describes seeing, with the pale skin and the large eyes and whatnot, except that this alien had a third eye on his forehead. And she also saw a security/surveillance camera with an eyeball as its lens and then a more elaborate picture of what appeared to be a ritual sacrifice. Three children were tied to stakes in front of a large crowd of men in military fatigues and business suits; some of the men dressed in elements of both uniforms, like a pair of camouflage pants topped by a white dress shirt and tie or a Purple Heart on a civilian blazer with a dress shirt above chino pants and combat boots. Shit like that. Several of these guys had rifles, and they shot the kids dead. Everything else she saw was essentially indescribable, just weird images in motion.

"After a while he was completely clear-headed while she was still kinda tripped-out, and they were hungry so he drove them to a taqueria. On the way they were listening to a custom-made mix of mellow-ish instrumental hiphop, including Jel, Omid, and Dosh, when she announced that rap was based on a cyclical sense of time, hence the frequently repetetitious nature of its production. According to her insight, each repeated musical sequence, such as a looped sample over a drum pattern, was akin to a microcosm of an entire timeline. Every four-bar loop or what-have-you is like the life-span of a universe or an amoeba, briefly running its course and then ending or dying and being replaced by an identical successor."

"That's some deep, trippy stuff, but I think I get it. It's like DJ Premier and

Odd Nosdam are channeling a genetically embedded understanding of quantum mechanics," I interject.

"Something like that," Chris replies. "Anyway, the story goes a level deeper after they get to the Mexican restaurant. Jessica was steadily returning to the real world but still kinda rambling about her experience while at the table they had chosen near a window. Both of them insist that they were speaking quietly enough that no one else in the place should have been able to understand what they were saying, yet another patron, a man with salt-and-pepper hair who didn't smile, walked up to their table and asked whether they had seen 'anything interesting out there today.' Maybe he could see the trippiness in their eyes from across the room. I don't know. They replied that they had.

"'Did you meet the Lizard Prince?' he wondered.

"'No, I don't think so,' Jessica said.

"'One summer I lived down in Tucson, this was a long time ago,' he said, 'and I took peyote one afternoon and wandered around for a bit, despite the heat, in the desert just outside the city. Some shrub caught my eye, and I fixated on it for what seemed like a moment or two. Then I heard a voice, except it didn't seem as though I were hearing it so much as having it inside my head. It had a strange quality that made it sound not totally human.

"'The voice said, 'One day, should you live long enough and continue to travel and converse with strangers, you can expect to meet someone who has seen the Lizard Prince in the desert. I cannot tell you where he is, because I do not know myself, but a few fortunate wanderers see him from time to time. Among those few are a few who are able to look the lizard in his right eye and view something that tells them the true nature of human civilization.'

"'This has intrigued me ever since,' the stranger told my friend and his girlfriend, 'because even before that I was, more or less, obsessed with the problems of human society and conflicted about whether these problems were consequences of human nature or of human habit.'

"Jessica told him about her hallucinations, which held his attention, and he informed her and Vince that her story would help him on his wisdom quest. Then the grim-faced stranger walked out the door, climbed into a sedan, and drove off."

"That was intense," I say to Chris, not knowing how properly to respond to such a narrative. "This occasion calls for a couple of beers."

I open my cooler and pull out the two brews I've brought. We sip our ales and listen to the end of the ballgame, then Chris stands, extends his hand for a solid shake, and says, "It's been great hanging with you, but I think I should get back to my campsite. Maybe we'll run across each other again some day."

"Yeah, maybe we will," I respond as he begins to stroll down the dirt path.

I hit the sleeping bag soon after and have a crazy, weird dream. In my dream I am in an operating room, watching a surgeon prepare for a procedure on a man with no mouth. Actually, that is a complete lie. I have no crazy, weird dream tonight. I have no dream of any sort, in fact, just like nearly every night of my life. Sometimes I feel that I'm missing out on something important, or at least interesting, when everyone else has these strange or funny nocturnal hallucinations while I have nothing to speak of. Bleubird, for our official e-interview, stated, "Last night I had a dream that a group of friends and I had to fight a Jamaican posse to the death; there was no good reason for the fight, but there was no stopping it either. Each group started in a garage full of weaponry, there was to be no guns...only bats, machetes, knives, sticks, chains, etc. I spent the entire time choosing the perfect combination of weapons and missed the fight. My friends died." And 'Bird is clearly a skilled musician. Mikah Nine has informed me that once "I had a dream I was able to see in all directions and see through anything I looked at" and is able to see through any beat and hit it from any direction he wants. Although I have had a few odd dreams and once dreamed that I literally had a third eye, I would never produce anything like the occasional dream sequences in *The Sopranos* or the opening song on Mr. Lif's *I Phantom* while sleeping. Do androids dream of electric sheep? I do not know. This mandroid dreams of nothing worth mentioning.

On the second day of my camping doubleheader I crack open a good book to accompany my cup of tasteless, free coffee. It's a potboiler by Noam Chomsky entitled *Imperial Ambitions*, a real page-turner, definitely some light summer reading. Some say that compromise is an art. Here I sit on vacation, nearly resigned to accepting that humanity will become prematurely extinct, possibly by the end of this century, without a grand revolutionary uprising, but, at least, my mind is staying sharp with the latest Chomsky. More than three years after the "cakewalk" war with Iraq was declared and the fucking thing continues, and I have long since abandoned the idea that I might make some contribution toward stopping the bloodshed. I participated in about half a dozen massive anti-war protests in San Francisco and Oakland despite a gut feeling that we (the protestors) would effect no change in the decisions of the insulated autocrats. Compromise is not an art for the likes of us. It's an acceptance of getting fucked over.

I recently dug up an underground gem called "Deus Ex Machina" by a Buffalo MC named 3rd Son, who speculates, in reference to the Bush administration, that "if life's a bitch, then karma's a motherfucker"; if that holds true—though I do not believe in karma or anything similar myself— then karma must have something brutal in store for the architects of this mass human slaughter as well as their soldier-enablers and propagandist-apologists. And, while my mind is on the topic of propagandists, I put away the book for a while and open the daily newspaper, which offers, among other things, a regular dose of right-wing ideology from local stalwart Michael Harmon, whose latest arrangement of ink concerns itself, as is typical, with defending the ever-threatened Rightist power structure that currently controls all three branches of the federal government. My father likes to joke that Harmon is just a bit to the left of Mussollini, while my brother and I have held that nationally syndicated pundit Cal Thomas may actually be further to the right than the local ideologue. Now would be a great time for a flashback...

Spring, 2004. A magical time. The aforementioned Harmon has delivered another Rightist missive to the unsuspecting readers of the *Portland Press Herald*, this time in the form of a suggested speech for Commander-in-Chief Bush, who apparently should have addressed the nation and essentially declared that he would do whatever the fuck he wanted, the critics be damned, and then closed with an invocation of the Christian god.

I fired off a missive in response, directly to this bonehead's e-mail address.

"Wow, you really put enough spin on that one to avoid any substantial honesty. First of all, you can't have a War on Terror. Warfare itself is a form of terrorism. When 'our' government slaughters civilians and destroys homes and infrastructures, it's called 'war.' When some group without an official license does the same thing, it's called 'terrorism.' And I think you need to study a little Afghan history..." and so on. I conclude with, "[a]nd how should Bush address the open possession of a massive arsenal of WMDs by his regime and the leaders of various US allies? 'Do as we say, not as we do'? God bless the United States, indeed."

To which Mr. Harmon replies, wittily, "Warfare is a form of terrorism? How is the weather on Mars?"

Trying to keep this discussion from descending into utter nonsense, I counter, "I'm from Mars? That's a great response to the points I made in my e-mail. I guess you could hardly respond to my argument without actually doing some research and independent thought, so resorting to that old standby of desperation known as 'reduction to an absurdity' was your best option....the overlap between any standard definitions of 'war' and 'terrorism' is so extensive that one must at least wonder if there's any significant difference between the two phenomena other than the parties perpetrating them."

After obviously giving the matter much thought, Harmon replies, "I have been refuting opinions such as yours for 14 years now. A detailed reply to what you write will be available when I publish my collected works." (I continue to await, breathlessly, this omnibus.)

And now I return from the whimsical past to the dreary present. I foresee another bitter winter in the hinterlands. looking up at zero degrees, you have to keep moving in the northeastern tundra or your feet will freeze where you stand. That's why I must enjoy this brief, sunny respite from frigidity; if I do not, then in January I will have no reminiscences to warm my cold blood. Even the least exciting afternoon at the beach or the lake seems like paradise when you're shoveling your driveway out after a blizzard and the only person keeping you company is some rapper who has a song echoing in your skull—once, for example, I could not shake Sage's "Dance Monkey" from my cranium while attempting to free my car from the depths of snow in the parking lot at my workplace—and the next summer seems like an event that may never happen.

When I'm feeding money-hungry hounds or moving snow mounds or enduring what I know to be personal deceit or doing the wake-work-sleep-repeat waltz on exhausted feet, I assume I never sold my hopes because I never got a receipt. Music is the salve I have for these and other wounds as we march in cell-phone-holding lock-step to a convenient doom. Awareness of our mortality makes life feel like a foisted scam, but despondency can never hoist my plans. I guess you have to find a few true assets to console yourself while you're trapped in plastic, examine every aspect, and learn each facet. I keep my face placid while my mind is like pumping rapids.

I decide to play (quietly) one of my many custom-made mix CDs, this one a compendium of West Coast indie-label rap, and as I look over the track list I realize that many of these songs come from illicit mp3 downloads. Until recently, I had virtually no applied ethics for my practice of exchanging mp3s through peer-to-peer online networks (starting with Napster and Kazaa before moving to Soulseek and bit-torrent ish) and considered complaints that this activity constituted theft to be ridiculous and pointless. Most of the recordings I obtained this way were from major-label artists who hardly needed my money added to the disgusting amount of wealth they had accumulated (and often flaunted), but when I did download a free copy of an M.F. Doom album or a Clutch song I felt no pang of conscience. Now I feel somewhat differently about the matter and have come to the sort of position that one might expect of Scribe at his best.

My change of opinion was, fittingly enough, initially sparked by an online discussion at a small-label stalwart's Web site. Sole started a forum topic at his site (www.soleone.org) and launched into a semi-invective, revelatory commentary on the phenomenon of file-sharing programs that actually made me reconsider whether I was engaging in unethical behavior when I procured music without remunerating the musicians. In his manifesto he mentions "a friend who released a record, hired radio and press people to work his record, got decent distribution, and still hasn't recouped all his costs; everyone he knows has a CD-R of his album and 'loves it.'" Sole's essential conclusion, buried among personal recollections of both traveling far out of his way to get indy-label records and scoffing at anti-mp3 arguments, is that "nothing is free, and if you love someone's music, you should support it."

Later in the discussion, after a number of his fans have posted their responses to his declaration, Sole boldly predicts, "the result of this all, will be in the near future, when there is no indy anything, and everybody is a subsidiary of something huge and everything sounds the same and is watered down to the point music isn't worth downloading anymore, I can assure you, the bedroom artists will try very hard to fill the void, but if people have this attitude of entitlement, that music is 'free for all,' even the bedroom hobbyists will get bored or burned out and when people do want to start a new indy renassaince, there won't be any indy distributors left, or indy labels, or indy fans."

Boston-area rapper-producer K-The-I (signed to Mush) adds, "[p]eople tell me that they got my CD and how dope it is, but I haven't even released it."

New Yorker LIFE-Long, in a 2004 interview with online hiphop magazine *Urban Smarts* (www.urbansmarts.com), takes a nuanced view of the issue: "Hey everybody wants a sneak preview. It's a problem when all cats do is share files and download and not support the artists. Especially the independent artists, because we have to sell records to eat. We don't get million dollar advances like some of these puppets in the game right now!"

Anyway, I decided to go to the catalyst of Sole's angst. Bleubird, the artist Sole used as a case where file-sharing harms the indy-music structures and a guy I'd met years earlier and more recently interviewed for my book, ought to make some sort of statement. And he does..."I for one don't download, but I'm quick to rip onto my computer or burn a CD so what's the difference?...I buy when I can and do my best to support. I understand sometimes our music is hard to find and some people use Soulseek to get their ears on it before they can get their hands on it. I just believe that for a label like Endemik, downloading means the difference between 2000 and 7000 records sold, and for people like me and [Endemik partner] Scott, who work multiple jobs to ensure that our music is released , it hits us directly in the pockets and stunts our growth as a label. If I were to step to a bigger label for their money the heads who would call me a 'sellout' are the same people who would just [as soon] download my record. When I sell a CD online I literally go out and buy lunch with that money."

Cage raps "I'll never get a platinum plaque for mp3s" on the Weathermen compilation *Conspiracy*, which I downloaded in '03 without paying a penny. However, I bought all three of his solo albums. I am starting to wonder if I did something detrimental to the independent-music system that I hold sacred when I got copies of that Weathermen project, an Anti-Pop Consortium album, two MF Doom albums, and various other alternative-label offerings and gave nothing back. Of course, I've paid for an abundance of recordings over the years and would hardly consider myself a leech; meanwhile all of the mainstream songs and LPs I've downloaded or burned have resulted in no guilt, even now. And it's unlikely that I ever will feel guilty about "illegally" duplicating a Led Zeppelin or Jay-Z disc, considering my ambivalence about whether mutherfuckers like them earn as much money as they receive and my non-ambivalence about whether they need my money added to their piles. Furthermore, I would contend that it runs counter to the interests of sustaining and nurturing an independent infrastructure when one diverts revenue to the corporate parasites instead of supporting a diverse array of innovative alternatives. In an era when mainstream rap is becoming less distinguishable from musical advertising (I have long wondered whether any rappers get compensated by any of the brand names they drop voluminous references to in their songs, partly because the entire absurdity reminds me of the paid product placements we see in big-budget movies) and the old rock heroes who haven't died are millionaires (for example, I seem to remember that David Bowie took his publishing company public and issued stocks), set within a larger economic context of increasing corporate consolidation and capital concentration, to maintain a variety of good-quality music and an effective distribution network for it is an overlooked quality-of-life struggle. If we lose access to good music in the ongoing process of Walmart-ization, everyday life will be that much less tolerable. I have arrived at a new personal code of conduct, which prohibits me from contributing to the demise of the network of minor labels and non-Fortune-500 distributors either by not paying for readily-available musical products or by lining the pockets of wealthy executives and shareholders by sticking my hard-earned scrills into the mainstream vacuum. True, we cannot escape from authoritarian tyranny through consumerism of any sort, but, for someone like me, life under capitalism is significantly more bearable if I have some great rap and rock to enlighten me.

I am well aware that this entire project has portrayed the indie-label system in some very flattering light, and a candid caveat is probably apropos. I should not give anyone the impression that the indie labels and distributors, the "mom-and-pop" retailers, or the smaller venues and show promoters are shining examples of highly ethical behavior, mainly because the individuals who operate this system often are as willing to engage in financial chicanery as the grifters of the major-label system. The smaller businesses still use a capitalistic modus operandi, though they tend to be less able to screw over musicans. Two other factors help the public perception of the "little guy" in the rap industry: some of the labels are founded by some of the musicians on their respective rosters; also, smaller labels, distributors, stores, promoters, and venues generally are more willing to take a risk on more creative music than their more affluent counterparts. I'd rather not get sued for libel, but I think I can get away with calling out, um, Mawkus Records (for allegedly not paying certain artists their hard-earned money) as well as, uh, Actmerk and Gush (for similar allegations) and a presumably defunct indie distributor whose name consists of three letters (for the same reason, remarkably enough) and an online retailer discussed elsewhere (for purportedly not delivering all of the merchandise its customers had paid for during its last months of operation). I hope no one confuses my acclaim for the artists of the underground/indie scene with praise for the petit bourgeouisie.

And now I sigh, stare into the horizon, and envision my microphone. It gently weeps, neglected and tucked away in the small basement of my two-bedroom duplex apartment. My old rhyme book lays prone on my computer desk, awaiting me through 40-hour work weeks that stack atop each other like the cement blocks of a prison. The day-to-day maintenance lifestyle of a modern North American poverty-wage earner hardly offers potential for growth as an artist in any field.

But enough about me. I practically shudder when I realize that I intended to put some finishing touches to my book, that undying monster that has haunted my life for two and a half years now, yet I have accomplished nothing thus far. Will this monstrosity never see its end and let me rest?

I pull out some printed pages of raw material from a folder in my car and peruse them to refresh my memory, noting the elements of each document that I may use in the last chapter or two of my opus. Astronautalis lists (smog) and Devin the Dude as musical inspirations, which is not too surprising, and then claims to admire Donald Rumsfeld, which I think is serious but cannot help but suspect is possibly meant to be an ironic joke at the government-bashing Scribe's expense. Bren, er, Alias in 2004 discusses his support for the candidacy of John Kerry, predicated on his hope that a Democrat would restore some of the education spending and military-veteran benefits slashed, with negative effects on Alias's wife and father, by G.W. Bush's administration. I reminisce on my failure, for two years, to sample the military-training record that Jel would eventually center his *Greenball 2* on and pontificate about my girlfriend's connections to the U.S. armed forces, mostly consequences of attending a high school with a military recruitment center literally across the street. (Also, her grandfather fought in Vietnam, and it has became obvious to me from our conversations that he feels that the bloodshed has dehumanized him to some extent.) I read my statement that during the purportedly liberal Bill Clinton's so-called humanitarian war in Yugoslavia children were murdered by NATO pilots who dropped bombs on houses and that pseudo-progressives like Mike Moore and Howard Dean contend that Iraq and Vietnam are examples of "bad wars" and are "mistakes" or "failures" when in fact they are achievements for the empire and no war is ever justified.

Elsewhere, K-The-I??? mentions Bjork, Portishead, and The Orb as musicians he is feeling and refers to nary a rap act, and he incriminates himself as an adult in the possession of a Transformers collection. I find a note reminding me to write a chapter entitled "MC Shitforlyrics and the Rap Republican Go Shopping." Also, some notes on a possible essay on the male-dominated nature of the rap underground and about the glaring lack of a female perspective in *my* writing about it; while Jean Grae, T-Love, Sontiago, Alexandrah, and Medusa have made meaningful contributions to the indie-rap canon, they are dwarfed by the number of guys in the field. Plus there is an implausible-but-true anecdote from 1999: an acquaintance named Heather and I were in Los Angeles and Santa Monica—I to visit, she to move—and she, for reasons I no longer remember, really wanted to connect with the Los Angeleno emcee Subtitle, whose phone number she did not have; one should keep in mind that L.A. County has a population of several million, relatively few of whom walk any distance greater than one block, and I was in the area for a total of two or three days; while we were waiting at a traffic light none other than Subtitle walked by my idling vehicle.

How am I to tie all of this material together? I cannot think of any logical way to fit these disparate pieces into my book as it stands, yet I would rather not waste them. There must be some device, however awkward and obvious, I can employ for this situation before I proceed to writing the conclusion and postscript.

Conclusion? Oh, right...I have none. This is not a strictly scholarly tome, though it includes intellectual elements and certainly required some scholarship; I need not wrap it in some thesis-ribbon. The planets aren't aligned, I may never make a dime, and my star may never shine, but at least this work is mine.

Postscript (for literal-minded readers)

The chapters on Mandrake, "the elusive hiphop backpacker" and paranormal communication via music and my PC are works of fanciful fiction. The pseudo-scholarly chapter with all of the footnotes is a parody; "Pious in the House of the Lord" is satirical. The piece about the deaf musician concerns a specific rapper. My investigation of the "white-supremacy rap scene" should be self-explanatory, as should certain segments of the "lists" chapter and the appendix. That bus ride really happened. The "Coda" is a combination of fiction and nonfiction. These pieces were composed between the fall of 2003 and the spring of March, 2007.

As I was proofreading and editing this book, an inside source at an unnamed major record label provided me with the pie chart (reproduced on the next page) that, he claims, he photocopied and smuggled out of the company's main office in Manhattan after a meeting of about one dozen top record industry executives. I found it quite revealing.

who gets what cut of that CD sale

Appendix: An Underground Insider's Glossary for Outsiders

Note: some readers may find themselves baffled or, at least, slightly unsure of their mastery of the hiphop vernacular and its underground/indie/DIY subset diction. Hence this handy little guide.

advance: *n*, funds provided to a musician upon signing a recording contract, purportedly to pay for the costs of recording, mixing, etc., but generally to support a lifestyle endowed with cannabis smoke and free of regular employment

Amityville: *n*, the city of Detroit, Michigan, also known as *Motor City*, *Motown* or *the Capital of Air Pollution Fetishism*

art-fag: *n*, mythical creature alleged to manufacture effeminate hiphop or hiphop-influenced music

ATL: *n*, the city of Atlanta, Georgia, the hiphop capital of the Southeast U.S. and cultural capital of the Dirty South

avant-gardist rap: *n*, forefront of the hiphop underground, consisting of those not afraid of musical progress; also known as *prog-rap*

baller: *n*, one who can afford to pay the bills in an age of stagnant incomes and accelerated costs of living

bangin': *adj*, voluptuous, curvaceous, fuckable, as in *damn, that female is bangin'*

beat: *n*, drum pattern(s), which provide(s) the backbone of nearly every hiphop track ever recorded; the element of a hiphop song that entices the listener to nod the neck or to call the police and complain about the noise

beatsmith: *n*, hiphop producer

bent: *adj*, drunk; *see MF Doom's classic "Dead Bent" for proper usage*

bite: *v*, to plagiarize or stylistically emulate

blackball: *v*, to ostracize of exclude without just cause, as in *Scribe has been blackballed from indie-rap's retail establishment for no apparent reason* blow up: *v*, to become commercially successful

boom-bap: *n*, general sound of an amplified drum pattern, esp. as heard from behind walls which inadvertantly protect the auditory organs

bounce: *v*, to exit; synonymous with *jet*, *merk*, and *get the fuck out*

Bricks, The: *n*, the city of Newark, New Jersey, also known as *the Fruit of the Garden State*

broseph: *n*, white male who uses the term *bro* as his preferred term of address

bump: *v*, to play any music loud enough to share with others who may not have been aware of their need to hear such music

Chi-Town: *n*, the city of Chicago, Illinois, sometimes called the Windy City*

chondriac: *adj*, excited or liable to become so

chops: *n*, rapid or staccato vocal cadence, rarely understood or appreciated by the many ignoramuses who prefer party jams composed by androids

Christian rap: *n*, genre of hiphop, sometimes affiliated with the underground, in which lyricists proclaim allegiance to a patriarchal deity who is simultaneously himself and his son and allegedly communicated with several prophets who may or may not have existed

cracker: *n (vulgar)*, white person, usu. one who is a racist, a cop, or a boss but occ. used in reference to an unknown white person in certain neighborhoods at certain times

crew: *n*, loose conglomeration of individuals assembled for the purposes of consuming alcohol, smoking marijuana, cracking jokes, and occasionally composing music

cut: *n*, song; *v*, synonymous with *scratch*

david: *adj*, moot

deal: *n*, recording contract (esp. with a major label), the Holy Grail for most of those who are underground

def: *adv*, definitely, as in *most def*

dirt hustle: *n*, low-paying vocation, such as marijuana sales or underground-rap artistry

Dirt Mall: *n*, the town of Standish, Maine

Dirty South, The: *n*, the southern region of the United States

dis: *v*, to expend one's finite creative energy on insulting the competition

DIY: *adj*, do-it-yourself; pertaining to a creation not financially supported by a formal business entity

DJ: *n*, (deejay or disc jockey) one who plays the musical recordings created by others and in return receives money, sexual access, and/or alcohol

dome piece: *n*, head, brain, or skull, each of which is responsible for the creation, propagation, and subsequent co-optation, usu. by squares, of the terms in this lexicon

dope: *adj* (*archaic*), of premium musical quality

dub: *v*, to make an unauthorized duplication of a recording and thereby enable the musician(s) responsible to remain hungry and thus artistically authentic

dun: *n*, any person who is being referred to or addressed

dust: *n*, PCP; shortened term for *angel dust*, also known by several other names, mostly coined by Cage and Tame One

emo: *adj*, emotive or emotional, pertaining to the form of rap whose practitioners do not promote sociopathic behavior in their lyrics

fall off: *v*, to cease to create relevant music and/or to cease to sell significant numbers of units

flow: *n*, the style of a rapper's vocal delivery

Floydean: *adj*, of or resembling in some fashion the music of Pink Floyd

Forest City: *n*, the city of Portland, Maine

four elements of hiphop, the: *n*, the disciplines of hiphop culture as embodied by the MC, the DJ, the graffiti artist, and the marketing executive

freestyle: *v*, to rap in an improvisational mode or to pretend to do so fresh: *adj*, possessing qualities pleasing to the senses, esp. the auditory sense; antonymous with *wack*; synonymous with *hot, blazing, off the hook, off the chain, off the ringer, illmatic, ultramagnetic, nasty, ill, sick* or *pretty good*

fuck: *v*, to engage in sexual intercourse with or steal from; *int, note: no meaning known for this word when used as an interjection*

fucked: *adj*, cheated

fucked up: *adj*, drunk, high, hallucinating, insane, or strange

fun dip: *n*, cocaine in its powder form, as in *coming down from that fun dip was not fun*

gonna: *v*, going to; *note: this is not a hiphop-specific verb, but the lexicographer felt the need to clarify and make official any use of this contraction*

goth: *adj*, dark, gloomy, or macabre in lyrical themes

Hell-A: *n*, the city of Los Angeles, California, also known as the City of Lucifer's Angels, or Los Angeles County and its cities, inc. Tinseltown, the LBC, C-Arson and Compton

hiphop poet: *n*, lyricist whose skill is generally in inverse proportion to his/her pretention and who secretly aspires to become either a respected poet or a genuine rapper

hook: *n*, hiphop song's chorus, oft. inc. references to drug use or boasts of the rapper's superiority to unspecified rivals

Illadelph: *n*, the city of Philadelphia, Pennsylvania, also known as *Philly*, named after the cigar

indie: *adj*, also spelled *indy*; independent; located somewhere between *underground* and *mainstream*, usu. used in reference to record labels and artists and sometimes used as a transfer point one way or the other

irony: *n*, occurrence wherein a writer misuses and/or belabors a literary term, rendering it hackneyed and virtually useless

jenny: *n*, white chick

jock: *v*, to enjoy conspicuously the products of a given artist

keystyle: *v*, to feign the ability to rap with the use of a personal computer and an Internet connection

knucklehead: *n*, person in possession of a superior intellect, as in *only a knucklehead would consult a glossary of slang*

loop: *n*, artfully or annoyingly repeated sample of a musical phrase

mainstream: *n*, the commercially dominant sector of the hiphop industry; *adj*, of or pertaining to the mainstream*

MC (emcee): *n*, rapper, esp. one who tries to present himself as more skilled than other rappers by virtue of his chosen self-description; variously, microphone controller, master of ceremonies, microphone checker, or mover of the crowd; also synonymous with *rhymer, rhymester, rhymesayer, rhyme slinger, rhyme spitter*, and *hiphop vocalist-writer who suffers from delusions of grandeur*

metaphor: *n*, simile; *note: this foolish sense of the term is hiphop-specific*

Natti: *n*, the city of Cincinnati, Ohio, also known as *Queen City* or *Cincy* or *Porkopolis*

nerd-rap: *n*; *note: this is a pejorative term with no known referent*

Oaktown: *n*, the city of Oakland, California, also known as *the Town, the Land*, or *the O* and possibly the greatest locale on Earth

peace: *int*, indication that one is ending a phone conversation, departing to visit one's girlfriend or mistress, or relocating to a social gathering with better drugs and more attractive women

pheta: *n*, crystal methamphetamine, also known as *meth, ice* or *speed*, a substance ingested to encourage one to perform household chores or to stay awake for nocturnal graffiti painting props: *n (archaic)*, respect or recognition, now routinely given to those who never received or earned any when this term had meaningful usage

psych-rap: *n*, hiphop music of a psychedelic propensity in lyrics, vocalism and/or instrumentation and, coincidentally, often produced and consumed by users of hallucinogens

punch in: *v*, to prove one's vocal talents by inserting, oft. obviously, re-recorded parts of verses, with the replaced parts sent to data limbo

puter: *n*, personal computer, the gift and the curse of underground rap

rap: *n*, hiphop music, as in *that cracker likes rap*; *v*, to sing-speak in rhythmic vocal styles, usu. accompanied by instrumental music, as in *that jackass doesn't know to rap*

rap group: *n*, formal conglomeration of musicians who follow the plans of a chosen leader in order to bask in the acclaim that results from his brilliance and/or labor; formal conglomeration of musicians who struggle under the control of a tyrant who gives commands and takes credit for the brilliance and/or labor of others

rap show: *n*, gathering of hiphop enthusiasts who pay to see a set of performances that starts an hour late, occ. features every musician scheduled to appear, and ends when venue employees politely escort patrons out of the building

rhymesmith: *n*, rapper; *note: the only known usage of this pretentious term is by the lexicographer himself*

ridiculoid: *adj*, ridiculous, ludicrous, absurdified, etc.

rip: *v*, to rap well

rock: *v*, to rap, esp. in the eastern United States

Rotten Apple, The: *n*, New York City and all of its squirming denizens; collectively, the five boroughs: Brooklyn (Crooklyn, BK or Bucktown), the Bronx (BX), Staten Island (Shaolin), Queens (Queens), and Manhattan (the

City), which includes Harlem (Uptown), a haven for upwardly mobile Euro-Americans

rubexlotroid: *n*, device located inside a microphone that interjects the term *yo* at the beginning of rap performances, whether in studio or on stage

Sacto: *n*, the city of Sacramento, California, also known as *Sac*, *Sactown*, and *the Home of the Three Strikes (against those too poor to afford good lawyers) Law*

salty: *adj*, upset or angry, as in *the producer was obviously salty after his groupmate referred to him as his DJ*

scratch: *v*, to manipulate a vinyl record, as done by a turntablist; *n*, sound created by turntablism

scrilla: *n*, money, also known as *scrills, cheddar, cake, dough/doe, cream, revenues, funds, lettuce, cabbage, fabrics, papers, trap, loot* or *stackola*, usu. by those who have comparatively little of it

Seatown: *n*, the city of Seattle, Washington, allegedly; also allegedly known as *Emerald City*

sellout: *n*, any dues-paid musician who signs a recording contract that potentially could lift him/her above the poverty line

serve: *v*, to defeat another rapper in a verbal contest by demonstrating the circular logic that one is superior because the other rapper is inferior

shammy: *n*, black chick

shithole: *n*, dingy venue; underpopulated city or town; end of a pen from which poor-quality writing flows

shrooms: *n*, psylocibin (psychedelic) mushrooms which, when ingested, induce hallucinations and inspire a not-insignificant portion of the underground rap canon

slang: *v*, to sell one's musical products (compact discs, etc.) without a traditional retail medium to the small number of hiphop fans capable of appreciating one's non-traditional music, although these fans will later accuse one of selling out or falling off when a greater number of fans come to appreciate one's music

sound man: *n*, ritual scapegoat for wack rap shows

spit: *v*, to rap, esp. in the western United States

splifted: *adj*, suffering from the ill effects of that scourge of humankind known as marijuana

spot: *n*, a place of social gathering or commerce

suck: *v*, to fail to possess any redeeming artistic qualities

Sucka Free: *n*, the city of San Francisco, California, also known as *Baghdad by the Bay*, *Ess Ef* and *San Fran*

tee-ar-cee: *v*, to steal from in a devious and stealthy, rather than upfront and menacing, manner

throw your hands up: *int*, invocation to a hiphop audience with the goal of inspiring excitement; *note: the repetition of this phrase may inspire one to want to throw one's lunch up*

titty: *n*, human breast, or, more properly, tit

turntablism: *n*, artful, bizarre, unique, oft. pointless manipulation of vinyl records with phonographs and mixers

Twin Cities, The: *n*, Minneapolis and St. Paul, Minnesnowta

underground: *n*, under-exposed, lower-budget hiphop scene; *adj*, of or pertaining to the underground, you dummy

viloporn: *n*, musical product fixated in its lyrics upon violence and gore; music with a sadomasochistic theme; the music of Eminem

wack: *adj*, not good but not "not good" in the manichean moral sense, i.e., bad but neither "evil" nor "bad" meaning "good"; synonymous with *sucky*, *crappy*, et al

wanna: *v*, want to; *note: this is not a hiphop-specific verb, but the lexicographer felt the need to clarify and make official any use of this contraction*

weed: *n*, marijuana, also known as *broccoli, green, ganja, spinach, boom, wool, mary, mary jane, the chronic, white girl,* or *The Stuff*

wigger: *n*, unabashed Euro-American fan of hiphop music

yo: *int*; *note: no definition known*

*Note: this definition is provided for ignoramuses only.

www.ingramcontent.com/pod-product-compliance
Lightning Source LLC
Chambersburg PA
CBHW032113090426
42743CB00007B/340